The Essence of Canada:A Travel Preparation Guide

Alexander Becker

TABLE OF CONTENTS

Introduction

Welcome to the land of breathtaking landscapes, vibrant cities, and warm hospitality—Canada, the second-largest country in the world, stretching from the Atlantic Ocean to the Pacific and reaching northward to the Arctic. This comprehensive travel guide will serve as your gateway to unlocking the wonders of this vast and diverse nation.

Canada is a land of extraordinary natural beauty, boasting majestic mountains, pristine forests, stunning coastlines, and an abundance of wildlife. But it's not just the awe-inspiring landscapes that make Canada a remarkable destination. Its multicultural cities, rich history, thriving arts scene, and friendly locals create a tapestry of experiences that will captivate travelers of all interests.

In this travel guide, we will embark on an unforgettable journey across Canada, exploring its distinct regions and uncovering the hidden gems that await. From the eastern shores of Newfoundland and Labrador to the picturesque beauty of British Columbia, from the cosmopolitan charm of Toronto to the French-speaking province of Quebec, Canada offers a plethora of adventures for every traveler.

CHAPTER ONE

•*About Canada*

Canada, known for its vast landscapes, diverse culture, and strong economy, is a fascinating country with a rich history. From its indigenous roots to its modern multicultural society, Canada has evolved into a nation that embraces both tradition and innovation. In this travel guide,we will explore various aspects of Canada, including its geography, history, culture, economy, and political system.

Geographically, Canada is the second-largest country in the world, spanning six time zones and stretching from the Atlantic to the Pacific Ocean. Its diverse terrain includes majestic mountains, pristine lakes, dense forests, and expansive prairies. Canada shares its southern border with the United States, forming the longest undefended border in the world.

The history of Canada is marked by the presence of indigenous peoples who inhabited the land long before European colonization. The First Nations, Inuit, and Métis peoples have distinct cultures and traditions that contribute to the country's multicultural fabric. The arrival of European explorers and settlers, primarily from France and Britain, led to the establishment of colonies and the eventual formation of the Dominion of Canada in 1867.

Canada's culture reflects the influences of its indigenous, French, and British heritage, as well as the contributions of immigrants from around the world. The country has two official languages, English and French, and its multiculturalism policy promotes the celebration and preservation of various cultural practices. Canadians take pride in their diverse cultural festivals, art, literature, music, and cuisine, which showcase the country's vibrant heritage.

The Canadian economy is highly developed and ranks among the largest in the world. With abundant natural resources, including minerals, oil, and timber, Canada has a thriving extractive industry. Additionally, the country is a major exporter of agricultural products such as wheat, canola, and maple syrup. Canada's service sector, encompassing finance, technology, healthcare, and education, is also a significant contributor to its economy.

Canada's political system is a parliamentary democracy and a constitutional monarchy, with Queen Elizabeth II as the reigning monarch. The country is divided into ten provinces and three territories, each with its own government. The federal government, located in Ottawa, is responsible for matters such as defense, foreign policy, and national infrastructure.

One notable aspect of Canada's political landscape in the early 2000s was the leadership of Prime Minister Jean Chrétien. Serving as the head of government from 1993 to 2003, Chrétien implemented policies aimed at reducing the national deficit and promoting social programs. His government also played a significant role in the negotiation and signing of the Kyoto Protocol, an international agreement on climate change.

In terms of international relations, Canada has a reputation for being a peacekeeping nation. It actively participates in United Nations peacekeeping missions and contributes to global humanitarian efforts. Canada's commitment to diplomacy, human rights, and multilateralism has helped shape its foreign policy and fostered positive relationships with countries around the world.

The early 2000s was a period of economic growth and technological advancement in Canada. The country experienced a booming housing market, low unemployment rates, and increased investments in research and development. The rise of the internet and digital technologies opened new opportunities for Canadian businesses and individuals, fostering innovation and entrepreneurship.

However, the early 2000s also posed challenges for Canada. The country faced debates and divisions over issues such as national unity, indigenous rights, healthcare reform, and environmental sustainability. These debates often sparked passionate discussions and highlighted the complexities of governing a diverse nation.

•*Why Visit Canada*

Canada, the second-largest country in the world, is a captivating land of breathtaking landscapes, vibrant cities, rich cultural heritage, and warm hospitality. As a diverse and expansive nation, Canada has always been a popular destination for travelers seeking unique experiences and unforgettable adventures. In this travel guide, we will delve into the myriad reasons why visiting Canada is an enticing proposition, focusing specifically on the year 2023.

Natural Splendors:
One cannot overstate the awe-inspiring natural beauty that Canada possesses. From the stunning Rocky Mountains to the vast forests of British Columbia, Canada's diverse landscapes offer endless opportunities for exploration and outdoor activities. Visitors can hike through pristine national parks, such as Banff and Jasper, marvel at majestic glaciers, or kayak in the crystal-clear waters of the Canadian Rockies. The country's commitment to environmental preservation and sustainable tourism ensures that visitors can witness these natural wonders in their unspoiled glory.

Wildlife Encounters:
Canada is a haven for wildlife enthusiasts and nature lovers. The country is home to a remarkable

array of species, including bears, moose, whales, and numerous bird species. In places like Churchill, Manitoba, visitors can observe the majestic polar bears in their natural habitat, or embark on a thrilling whale-watching expedition on the coasts of British Columbia. Canada's commitment to wildlife conservation allows visitors to witness these incredible creatures up close while ensuring their long-term protection.

Multiculturalism and Diversity:
Canada is renowned for its multicultural fabric, embracing a rich tapestry of cultures, languages, and traditions. The country's cities, such as Toronto, Vancouver, and Montreal, are vibrant melting pots where diverse communities thrive. Visitors can immerse themselves in cultural festivals, explore ethnic neighborhoods, savor global cuisines, and appreciate art and music from around the world. Canada's commitment to inclusivity and diversity creates an atmosphere of openness and acceptance that enriches the travel experience.

Urban Excursions:
While Canada's natural landscapes are truly awe-inspiring, its cities are no less captivating. The

country boasts several cosmopolitan hubs that offer a blend of history, modernity, and world-class amenities. Toronto, Canada's largest city, showcases iconic landmarks like the CN Tower and the Royal Ontario Museum, while Montreal enchants visitors with its European charm and vibrant arts scene. Vancouver enthralls with its stunning waterfront, Stanley Park, and proximity to nature, making it a gateway to outdoor adventures. These cities provide a diverse range of activities, including shopping, dining, cultural events, and nightlife, ensuring there is something for every visitor.

Adventure Sports:
For thrill-seekers, Canada offers a plethora of adventure sports and adrenaline-pumping activities. The country's topography and natural resources provide the perfect setting for activities like skiing, snowboarding, ice climbing, and dog sledding during the winter months. In the summer, visitors can go white-water rafting, mountain biking, hiking, or take part in aerial activities like zip-lining and paragliding. From the rugged coastlines of Newfoundland to the mountains of Whistler, Canada offers adventure sports for all skill levels and preferences.

Festivals and Events:

Canada's event calendar is brimming with festivals and celebrations that cater to a wide range of interests. From the Calgary Stampede, a world-renowned rodeo and exhibition, to the Montreal Jazz Festival, the largest jazz festival in the world, there is no shortage of cultural, music, and sporting events to enthrall visitors. Other notable events include Toronto's International Film Festival, Quebec Winter Carnival, and the Vancouver International Wine Festival. These events not only showcase Canada's vibrant culture and artistic prowess but also provide a platform for locals and tourists to come together and celebrate.

Historical and Cultural Heritage:

Canada's history is deeply rooted in indigenous cultures and the heritage of early European settlers. Throughout the country, visitors can explore historic sites, museums, and indigenous communities to gain a deeper understanding of Canada's past. Places like Québec City, with its well-preserved Old Town, and the Canadian Museum for Human Rights in Winnipeg, shed light on the nation's diverse heritage and historical significance. This exploration allows visitors to appreciate Canada's evolution and the contributions of its indigenous peoples.

Culinary Delights:

Canadian cuisine is a delectable fusion of diverse culinary traditions. From fresh seafood on the East Coast to poutine in Quebec and farm-to-table experiences in the fertile regions of British Columbia, food lovers are in for a treat. Visitors can embark on culinary tours, sample regional specialties, and indulge in world-class dining experiences. The country's booming craft beer and wine industry further enhance the gastronomic offerings, providing ample opportunities to savor local brews and exquisite wines.

•Travel Tips

Canada, the second-largest country in the world, is a land of breathtaking natural beauty, vibrant cities, and diverse cultural experiences. From the stunning Rocky Mountains to the picturesque coastlines, Canada offers a plethora of attractions for travelers to explore. To ensure a smooth and memorable journey, it is essential to plan ahead and be well-prepared. In this guide, we will provide you with valuable travel tips to help you make the most of your trip to Canada.

Entry Requirements:

Before embarking on your journey, familiarize yourself with the entry requirements for Canada. Most visitors need a valid passport to enter the country, while some may require additional documents such as a visa or an Electronic Travel Authorization (eTA). Ensure that your travel documents are up to date and meet the specific requirements for your country of origin.

Best time to visit:

Canada's climate varies greatly across its vast expanse, so choosing the right time to visit depends on your preferred activities and destinations. Summer (June to August) is the peak tourist season, offering pleasant weather and a myriad of outdoor activities. Winter (December to February) brings opportunities for skiing and snowboarding, particularly in regions like British Columbia and Alberta. Spring and autumn offer milder temperatures and fewer crowds, making them ideal for exploring cities and enjoying fall foliage.

Transportation:

Canada's expansive geography necessitates reliable and efficient transportation options. If you plan to visit multiple cities or provinces, consider flying between destinations to save time. Canada has a well-developed domestic flight network, connecting major cities and remote regions alike. Alternatively, you can explore the country by train, with VIA Rail offering scenic routes across the nation. For shorter distances within cities, public transportation systems such as buses, subways, and trams are reliable and convenient.

Health and Safety:

While Canada is generally a safe country for travelers, it's essential to take precautions to ensure your well-being. Prior to your trip, check if your health insurance covers any medical emergencies while abroad. Carry a copy of your insurance policy and necessary prescriptions for any medications you require. It's also advisable to pack a basic first aid kit and familiarize yourself with emergency numbers in Canada. Be cautious when exploring remote areas, follow park regulations, and take necessary precautions while engaging in outdoor activities.

Currency and Payments:

The official currency of Canada is the Canadian dollar (CAD). It's recommended to carry a mix of cash and credit/debit cards. Credit cards are widely accepted in most establishments, but it's always wise to have some cash for smaller businesses or places that may not accept cards. ATMs are easily accessible in cities and towns, allowing you to withdraw cash in the local currency.

Accommodation:

Canada offers a range of accommodation options to suit various preferences and budgets. From luxury hotels to budget-friendly hostels and cozy bed and breakfasts, there is something for everyone. When booking accommodations, consider factors such as location, amenities, and reviews from previous guests. It's advisable to book in advance, especially during peak travel seasons, to secure your preferred accommodations.

Canadian Culture and Etiquette:

Canada is known for its multiculturalism and friendly inhabitants. Respect for diversity and cultural differences is highly valued. Canadians are generally polite and reserved, so it's important to be courteous and considerate in your interactions. Tipping is customary in Canada, typically ranging from 15% to 20% of the total bill in restaurants, bars, and taxis. Familiarize yourself with local customs and traditions to ensure a positive and respectful experience.

Must-See Attractions:
Canada boasts numerous iconic attractions that should not be missed. Some notable highlights include Niagara Falls, the stunning Rocky Mountains, the historic city of Quebec, the cosmopolitan city of Toronto, the charming coastal villages of the Maritimes, and the picturesque landscapes of the Canadian Rockies. Research the attractions that align with your interests and plan your itinerary accordingly.

Outdoor Adventures:
Nature enthusiasts will be enthralled by Canada's outdoor adventures. From hiking in national parks to kayaking in pristine lakes and spotting wildlife, the country offers a wealth of opportunities for outdoor exploration. Research and plan your outdoor activities in advance, ensuring you have the necessary equipment, permits (if required), and knowledge of safety guidelines.

Local Cuisine:

Canadian cuisine is as diverse as its population. Be sure to savor some iconic Canadian dishes, such as poutine (fries with cheese curds and gravy), butter tarts, Nanaimo bars, and Montreal-style bagels. Don't miss the opportunity to try regional specialties like smoked salmon in British Columbia or tourtière in Quebec. Explore local farmers' markets for fresh produce and indulge in the country's thriving culinary scene.

CHAPTER TWO

Planning Your Trip

•*Best Time to Visit Canada*

Canada boasts diverse landscapes, vibrant cities, and a rich cultural heritage. From the breathtaking Rocky Mountains to the stunning Niagara Falls, Canada offers a multitude of attractions for travelers. However, with its vast territory spanning six time zones, choosing the ideal time to visit can be a challenging task. This travel guide aims to guide prospective travelers by highlighting the best time to visit Canada, taking into account the country's climatic variations and seasonal attractions.

Spring;
Spring in Canada, which spans from March to May, is a magical time when nature awakens from its winter slumber. During this season, the weather gradually warms up, and colorful blooms start to appear across the country. One of the most popular springtime events is the annual Cherry Blossom Festival in Vancouver, where the city is adorned with delicate pink cherry blossoms. Additionally, in

eastern Canada, the iconic tulip festivals in Ottawa and Montreal showcase vibrant displays of tulips, symbolizing the country's enduring friendship with the Netherlands. Spring is also an excellent time to visit the national parks, such as Banff and Jasper, before the summer crowds arrive. However, it's important to note that weather conditions can be unpredictable in the early spring months, so packing layered clothing is advisable.

Summer;

Summer, from June to August, is arguably the most popular time to visit Canada. The country comes alive with festivals, outdoor activities, and pleasant temperatures. Coastal regions, like Vancouver Island and the Maritimes, enjoy milder summers, making them ideal for exploring charming seaside towns and indulging in water sports. The Canadian Rockies offer breathtaking vistas and countless hiking trails for outdoor enthusiasts. Wildlife lovers can also witness the annual migration of whales along the Atlantic and Pacific coasts. Furthermore, summer showcases the country's diverse cultural events, including the Calgary Stampede, a world-renowned rodeo and exhibition, and the Montreal Jazz Festival, attracting music aficionados from around the globe. However, it's essential to plan accommodation and activities well in advance, as summer is the peak tourist season, and popular destinations can get crowded.

Autumn;

Autumn, from September to November, is a visually captivating season in Canada, with landscapes transformed by vibrant hues of red, orange, and yellow. The country's vast forests, such as Algonquin Provincial Park in Ontario and Fundy National Park in New Brunswick, become a photographer's paradise. Visitors can partake in scenic drives, embark on hiking trails, or even enjoy boat cruises along rivers flanked by colorful foliage. Additionally, autumn is the perfect time to visit the picturesque wine regions of British Columbia and Ontario, where vineyards are filled with ripe grapes ready for harvest. The Okanagan Valley and Niagara-on-the-Lake offer wine tours and tastings amidst breathtaking surroundings. It's important to note that autumn weather can be unpredictable, so it's advisable to pack layers and be prepared for temperature fluctuations.

Winter;

For travelers seeking snow-covered landscapes and winter sports, Canada's winter season, from

December to February, provides a plethora of opportunities. The country offers world-class skiing and snowboarding resorts, including Whistler in British Columbia and Mont-Tremblant in Quebec. The province of Manitoba becomes a hub for witnessing the mesmerizing Northern Lights. Moreover, winter festivals, such as Quebec City's Winter Carnival and Ottawa's Winterlude, showcase the country's vibrant cultural heritage, featuring ice sculptures, outdoor concerts, and exciting winter sports competitions. However, it's crucial to be prepared for cold temperatures, especially in northern regions, and ensure appropriate winter gear is packed.

• VISA REQUIREMENTS

To ensure the integrity of its borders and facilitate safe and orderly travel, Canada has established visa requirements for foreign visitors. In this comprehensive guide, we will delve into the visa requirements to visit Canada, exploring different categories of visas, application procedures, and important considerations for travelers. Whether you are planning a short visit or a long-term stay, this guide will provide you with valuable insights and help you navigate the Canadian visa system.

Overview of Canadian Visa :
The Canadian visa system is designed to regulate the entry of foreign nationals into the country. The main types of visas include visitor visas, work permits, study permits, and permanent residency. For the purpose of this guide, we will primarily focus on visitor visas, which allow individuals to temporarily visit Canada for tourism, business, or family visits.

Visitor Visa Categories:
a. Temporary Resident Visa (TRV): The Temporary Resident Visa, commonly known as a visitor visa, is the most common visa category for short-term visits to Canada.It is required for citizens of countries that are not visa-exempt. This section will outline the eligibility criteria, application process, and necessary documents for obtaining a TRV.

b. Electronic Travel Authorization (eTA): Introduced in 2016, the eTA is an electronic travel authorization required for visa-exempt foreign nationals traveling to Canada by air. This section will detail the countries eligible for the eTA, application procedures, and important considerations.

Eligibility Criteria:

To be eligible for a Canadian visitor visa, applicants must meet certain requirements set by the government. These requirements typically include factors such as the purpose of the visit, financial capacity, ties to their home country, and intention to leave Canada after the authorized period of stay. This section will explore the eligibility criteria in detail, highlighting key factors that immigration officers consider during the application process.

Application Process:

a. Application Forms: This section will outline the different application forms required for visitor visas, including the Temporary Resident Visa Application (IMM 5257) and the Application for Electronic Travel Authorization (eTA).

b. Supporting Documents: A comprehensive list of supporting documents required for a visitor visa application will be provided in this section. These documents may include a valid passport, proof of financial support, travel itinerary, and more. Tips for preparing these documents and ensuring they meet the requirements will also be discussed.

c. Biometrics and Medical Examinations: In certain cases, biometric data collection and medical examinations may be necessary for visa applicants. This section will provide an overview of when and how these procedures are conducted.

Processing Times and Fees:
Understanding the processing times and fees associated with visa applications is essential for planning a trip to Canada. This section will explain the factors affecting processing times, provide an estimated timeline, and outline the visa application fees.

Visa Exemptions and Special Considerations: Certain individuals, such as citizens of visa-exempt countries, may be exempt from the requirement of obtaining a visitor visa. This section will explore visa exemptions, transit requirements, and special considerations for specific groups, such as minors, students, and business visitors.

Extending Your Stay and Changing Visa Status:

Visitors in Canada may sometimes wish to extend their stay or change their visa status while in the country. This section will discuss the options available for extending a visitor visa, applying for a work or study permit, or transitioning to permanent residency.

•Currency and Exchange Rates

When planning a trip to Canada, it is essential to familiarize yourself with the local currency and the prevailing exchange rate. This guide aims to provide a comprehensive overview of the currency system in Canada, including its history, denominations, security features, and tips for exchanging money. By understanding the Canadian dollar (CAD) and its exchange rate, travelers can better navigate financial transactions during their visit to this diverse and picturesque country.

I. History of the Canadian Dollar:
The Canadian dollar has a rich history, dating back to the early 17th century when the first European settlers arrived in Canada. Over time, various currencies were in circulation until 1858 when the Canadian dollar became the official currency. The

Bank of Canada, established in 1934, became responsible for issuing and regulating the Canadian dollar.

II. Currency Denominations:
The Canadian dollar is divided into cents, with coins available in denominations of 1 cent (penny), 5 cents (nickel), 10 cents (dime), 25 cents (quarter), and 1 dollar (loonie). Additionally, there is a 2-dollar coin called the "toonie." Banknotes come in denominations of 5, 10, 20, 50, and 100 dollars, each featuring notable Canadian personalities, landscapes, and symbols.

III. Security Features:
To ensure the integrity of the currency, Canadian banknotes incorporate various security features. These include holographic strips, raised ink, transparent windows, and unique serial numbers. Familiarizing yourself with these security features can help you distinguish between genuine banknotes and counterfeit ones.

IV. Current Exchange Rate:
The exchange rate determines the value of the Canadian dollar in relation to other currencies. It fluctuates daily and is influenced by factors such as

market demand, interest rates, and economic indicators. Travelers can check the current exchange rate through financial websites, banks, or currency exchange services. It is advisable to compare rates from different sources to ensure a fair exchange.

V. Exchanging Currency in Canada:

There are several options for exchanging currency in Canada. Travelers can use banks, credit unions, currency exchange offices, or automated currency exchange machines. Banks typically offer competitive rates, while currency exchange offices may charge higher fees. It is advisable to compare rates and fees before making a decision. Additionally, many businesses in Canada accept major credit cards, reducing the need for cash in certain transactions.

VI. Tips for Currency Exchange:

Plan ahead: It is advisable to exchange a small amount of currency before arriving in Canada to cover immediate expenses.

Research exchange rates: Stay informed about the current exchange rates to get the best value for your money.

Avoid exchanging currency at airports: Airport currency exchange services often charge higher fees and offer less favorable rates.

Notify your bank: Inform your bank or credit card provider of your travel plans to avoid any issues with card usage while in Canada.

Carry a mix of payment options: Carry a combination of cash, credit cards, and debit cards for flexibility.

VII. Using ATMs and Credit Cards:

ATMs are widely available in Canada and offer a convenient way to withdraw Canadian dollars using your debit or credit card. However, be aware that your bank may charge fees for international ATM transactions. It is advisable to inquire about these fees before using ATMs. Credit cards are widely accepted in most establishments, but it's essential to notify your credit card provider of your travel plans to avoid any card holds or limitations.

VIII. Currency Conversion Apps:

Consider installing a reliable currency conversion app on your smartphone. These apps can help you quickly convert prices from your home currency to the Canadian dollar, making it easier to understand costs and avoid unnecessary expenses.

•*Transportation in Canada*

To make the most of your Canadian adventure, it is essential to understand the transportation options available. This guide provides an overview of transportation in Canada, including air travel, trains, buses, ferries, and rental cars. Whether you are planning a cross-country road trip or seeking efficient ways to hop between cities, this guide will help you navigate the transportation system and enhance your travel experience.

I. Air Travel ;
Air travel is the most popular and convenient mode of transportation for long distances within Canada. With numerous domestic and international airports, it connects major cities and remote regions alike. Canada's primary airports include Vancouver International Airport, Toronto Pearson International Airport, and Montréal–Pierre Elliott Trudeau International Airport. Additionally, several regional airports serve smaller communities and tourist destinations.

Travelers can choose from several airlines operating domestic flights, such as Air Canada, WestJet, and Porter Airlines. These airlines offer comprehensive networks connecting major cities, making it easy to explore different regions of the country. It is recommended to book flights in advance, especially during peak travel seasons, to secure the best fares.

II. Trains;
Train travel in Canada provides a unique and scenic way to experience the country's vast landscapes. Via Rail is Canada's national passenger rail service, offering both long-distance and regional train routes. The flagship train, "The Canadian," runs from Toronto to Vancouver, spanning nearly 4,500 kilometers and providing breathtaking views of the Rocky Mountains.

The train service also connects major cities like Montreal, Ottawa, and Winnipeg, making it a convenient alternative to air travel for shorter distances. The train cabins are comfortable, equipped with amenities, and provide an opportunity to socialize with fellow travelers. However, it is important to note that train travel can be slower compared to air travel, so plan accordingly if time is a significant factor.

III. Buses and Coaches ;

Buses and coaches are a popular and economical means of transportation in Canada, particularly for shorter distances and regional travel. Companies like Greyhound, Megabus, and Coach Canada operate extensive bus networks connecting major cities and towns throughout the country.

Greyhound, for instance, offers a comprehensive network, making it possible to travel from coast to coast. Bus services are generally reliable and comfortable, with amenities like onboard Wi-Fi and power outlets. However, travel times can be longer compared to air or train travel, so consider this when planning your itinerary.

IV. Ferries;

Canada's extensive coastline and numerous islands offer exciting opportunities for ferry travel. British Columbia, with its intricate network of fjords and islands, provides an array of ferry routes. BC Ferries is the primary operator, connecting Vancouver Island to mainland British Columbia and other islands in the region.

In the Atlantic provinces, ferries are an integral part of the transportation system, connecting mainland Canada to destinations such as Prince Edward

Island and Newfoundland and Labrador. Marine Atlantic operates the ferry service between Nova Scotia and Newfoundland, offering both passenger and vehicle transportation.

V. Rental Cars ;
Renting a car is an excellent option for exploring Canada's vast landscapes and accessing remote areas. Major car rental companies like Avis, Budget, and Hertz have branches at airports and major cities across the country. Renting a car provides flexibility and allows you to set your own pace while traveling.

Canada has an extensive network of well-maintained highways, making road trips a popular choice for travelers. The Trans-Canada Highway stretches across the country, providing a scenic route for those looking to traverse the entire breadth of Canada. However, it is important to note that driving conditions can vary, especially during winter months, so be prepared and check weather and road conditions before embarking on your journey.

•Accommodation Options

Whether you're planning a visit to the breathtaking Rocky Mountains, the charming coastal towns, or the bustling metropolitan areas, finding suitable accommodation is essential for a memorable and comfortable stay. This comprehensive travel guide will provide you with an overview of the various accommodation options available in Canada, from luxurious hotels to budget-friendly alternatives, ensuring that you can make an informed choice based on your preferences and budget.

Hotels and Resorts:
Hotels and resorts are a popular choice for travelers seeking comfort, convenience, and a range of amenities. Canada offers a wide selection of accommodations, ranging from luxurious five-star hotels to boutique establishments, ensuring that every traveler can find a suitable option. Major cities like Vancouver, Toronto, and Montreal boast an array of high-end hotels with world-class facilities, including spa services, fine dining, and breathtaking views. Additionally, Canada is home to several renowned resort destinations, such as Whistler, Banff, and Mont Tremblant, where you

can indulge in outdoor activities while enjoying top-notch accommodations.

Bed and Breakfasts:

For a more personalized and intimate experience, consider staying at a bed and breakfast (B&B). B&Bs are often located in charming heritage homes or quaint cottages, offering cozy rooms and home-cooked breakfasts. These accommodations provide a unique opportunity to connect with local hosts and gain insider knowledge about the surrounding area. B&Bs are particularly popular in smaller towns and rural regions, where you can immerse yourself in the local culture and enjoy a warm, welcoming atmosphere.

Vacation Rentals:

Vacation rentals have gained immense popularity in recent years, providing travelers with the flexibility and convenience of a home away from home. Websites and platforms like Airbnb and VRBO offer a vast range of options, including apartments, condos, cottages, and even unique properties like treehouses and yurts. Vacation rentals are an excellent choice for families or groups, as they often offer multiple bedrooms, fully equipped kitchens, and additional amenities such as private pools or outdoor spaces. Whether you prefer a cozy apartment in the heart of a vibrant city or a secluded cabin in the wilderness, vacation rentals cater to a variety of preferences and budgets.

Hostels:
Ideal for budget-conscious travelers, hostels provide affordable accommodation options, particularly for solo travelers or those seeking a social atmosphere. Hostels are prevalent in major cities and popular tourist destinations, offering dormitory-style rooms with shared facilities such as kitchens, lounges, and communal areas. Some hostels also provide private rooms for those who prefer more privacy. In addition to the cost-saving benefits, hostels often organize social events, tours, and activities, making them a great choice for meeting fellow travelers and exploring Canada on a budget.

Campgrounds and RV Parks:
Canada's vast and breathtaking natural landscapes make it a paradise for outdoor enthusiasts. Camping is a popular way to experience the country's natural beauty, with numerous well-maintained campgrounds and RV parks scattered across the country. National and

provincial parks offer a range of camping options, from basic tent sites to fully serviced RV parks with amenities like electricity, water hookups, and showers. Camping allows you to immerse yourself in nature, enjoy activities like hiking and wildlife spotting, and stargaze under clear skies. It's important to note that camping facilities vary, so be sure to check availability, reservation requirements, and any specific regulations in advance.

Indigenous Accommodations:

For a unique and culturally immersive experience, consider staying at an Indigenous-owned accommodation. Indigenous communities across Canada offer opportunities to stay in traditional lodges, teepees, or longhouses, allowing visitors to learn about Indigenous culture, traditions, and history firsthand. These accommodations often provide cultural activities, guided tours, and the chance to engage with Indigenous hosts, making it a truly enriching experience for travelers interested in connecting with Canada's Indigenous heritage.

•*Travel Insurance*

Whether you are planning to explore the stunning Rocky Mountains, immerse yourself in the multicultural hub of Toronto, or embark on an adventure in the maritime provinces, it is crucial to prioritize your safety and well-being during your journey. Travel insurance serves as an indispensable companion, offering protection and peace of mind in the face of unforeseen events. In this comprehensive guide, we will explore the importance of travel insurance in Canada, its coverage options, and key considerations for selecting the right policy.

I. Why Travel Insurance Matters in Canada:

Medical Emergencies:
a. Access to High-Quality Healthcare: Canada boasts an excellent healthcare system, but as a non-resident, you may not be eligible for free medical services. Travel insurance ensures you receive prompt medical attention and covers expenses for emergency medical treatment, hospital stays, and prescription medication.
b. Protection against Costly Medical Bills: In the event of a medical emergency, the costs can escalate

quickly. Travel insurance safeguards you from exorbitant medical expenses, including ambulance services, medical evacuation, and repatriation.

Trip Cancellation and Interruption:
a. Reimbursement for Cancelled or Interrupted Trips: Unexpected circumstances like illness, accidents, or natural disasters can force you to cancel or cut short your trip. Travel insurance provides financial coverage for non-refundable expenses such as flights, accommodations, and pre-booked activities.
b. Coverage for Travel Delays: Travel insurance offers compensation for expenses incurred due to delayed flights or other travel-related mishaps, including accommodation, meals, and alternative transportation arrangements.

Lost, Stolen, or Damaged Belongings:
a. Protection for Personal Belongings: Travel insurance safeguards your personal belongings against theft, loss, or damage. This coverage includes luggage, electronics, and valuable items such as jewelry or cameras.
b. Emergency Cash and Document Assistance: In case of stolen or lost travel documents or money, travel insurance provides assistance in obtaining

emergency funds and replacing necessary documents.

II. Travel Insurance Coverage Options:

Medical Coverage:
a. Emergency Medical Expenses: This coverage encompasses emergency medical treatment, hospital stays, and prescription medication costs.
b. Medical Evacuation and Repatriation: Travel insurance ensures the safe transfer to a suitable medical facility or repatriation to your home country if medically necessary.

Trip Cancellation and Interruption Coverage:
a. Trip Cancellation: Reimbursement for non-refundable expenses in the event of trip cancellation due to covered reasons such as illness, injury, or death of a family member.
b. Trip Interruption: Financial protection for the unused portion of your trip if you need to return home early due to covered reasons.

Baggage and Personal Belongings Coverage:

a. Baggage Loss or Delay: Compensation for lost, stolen, or delayed luggage, including reimbursement for essential items purchased during the delay.

b. Personal Belongings: Coverage for theft, loss, or damage to personal items such as electronics, jewelry, and valuable belongings.

Emergency Assistance Services:

a. 24/7 Emergency Assistance: Access to a helpline for medical advice, coordination of medical services, and emergency assistance during your trip.

b. Travel Document and Cash Assistance: Help in replacing lost or stolen travel documents and provision of emergency cash.

III. Key Considerations for Selecting Travel Insurance in Canada:

Coverage Limits and Exclusions: Understand the coverage limits and exclusions specific to each policy, including pre-existing medical conditions, adventure sports, and high-value items.

Duration and Frequency of Travel: Consider whether you require single-trip or multi-trip insurance, based on the frequency and duration of your travel plans.

Deductibles and Premiums: Evaluate the deductibles and premiums associated with different policies to find a balance between affordability and comprehensive coverage.

Read the Policy Fine Print: Thoroughly review the policy terms, conditions, and limitations to ensure you are aware of the coverage provided and any requirements or obligations.

Reputation and Financial Stability: Choose insurance providers with a solid reputation, excellent customer service, and strong financial stability.

CHAPTER THREE

Exploring Canada's Cities

•*Toronto*

Toronto, the capital of Ontario and the largest city in Canada, is a dynamic metropolis that offers a plethora of attractions and experiences for travelers. This bustling city is renowned for its diverse culture, architectural marvels, world-class museums, vibrant neighborhoods, and a thriving culinary scene. Whether you're a history buff, a nature enthusiast, an art lover, or a foodie, Toronto has something for everyone. In this guide, we will delve into the highlights of this captivating city, providing you with a comprehensive guide for your Canadian travel adventure.

Historical and Cultural Gems:
Toronto boasts a rich history and is home to several iconic landmarks that showcase its cultural heritage. Start your exploration with a visit to Casa Loma, a magnificent castle built in the early 20th

century. This Gothic Revival mansion offers breathtaking views of the city skyline and houses an array of exhibits and artifacts. For a glimpse into Toronto's past, head to the Distillery District, a pedestrian-only village featuring Victorian-era industrial buildings converted into art galleries, boutiques, and restaurants.

To dive deeper into the city's diverse culture, visit the Royal Ontario Museum (ROM), one of North America's largest museums. The ROM showcases a vast collection of art, natural history, and cultural artifacts, including exhibits dedicated to Canadian history and indigenous cultures. Additionally, explore the Art Gallery of Ontario (AGO), which houses an extensive collection of Canadian and international artworks, including masterpieces by renowned artists like the Group of Seven and Pablo Picasso.

Neighborhoods and Cityscape :

Toronto is renowned for its distinct neighborhoods, each with its own unique character and charm. Begin with a stroll through the colorful streets of Kensington Market, a bohemian enclave filled with vintage shops, eclectic eateries, and vibrant street art. Move on to the trendy Queen West neighborhood, known for its hip boutiques, galleries, and lively nightlife.

No visit to Toronto is complete without experiencing the iconic CN Tower. Offering panoramic views of the city, this architectural marvel also features a revolving restaurant and an adrenaline-pumping EdgeWalk, where visitors can walk on a ledge outside the tower. Adjacent to the CN Tower is Ripley's Aquarium of Canada, showcasing a mesmerizing display of marine life, including sharks, jellyfish, and stingrays.

Another must-visit area is the revitalized waterfront district. Take a stroll along the Harbourfront, enjoy the serene beauty of Lake Ontario, and explore the vibrant Toronto Islands, a group of small islands offering beaches, picnic areas, and scenic bike trails.

Green Spaces and Nature :
Despite being a bustling urban center, Toronto is also blessed with numerous green spaces and natural retreats. High Park, the city's largest public park, spans over 400 acres and offers a perfect escape from the urban hustle. Explore its beautiful trails, visit the cherry blossom groves in the spring, or relax by Grenadier Pond.

For a truly unique experience, visit the Evergreen Brick Works, a former industrial site transformed into a hub for sustainability and nature education. This urban oasis features a picturesque quarry garden, hiking trails, and hosts farmers markets and cultural events.

Culinary Delights :
Toronto's diverse culinary scene reflects its multicultural population. From trendy food markets to fine dining establishments, the city offers a tantalizing array of flavors. St. Lawrence Market, a historic market housed in a 19th-century building, is a food lover's paradise. Indulge in local delicacies, sample international cuisine, or pick up fresh produce, cheeses, and meats.
To savor global flavors, head to Kensington Market, where you can find a variety of international cuisines, from Caribbean to Middle Eastern. Don't miss out on exploring the diverse range of Asian culinary offerings in Toronto's Chinatown and Koreatown.

Festivals and Events:
Toronto hosts a vibrant calendar of festivals and events throughout the year. In June, the city comes alive with the Toronto Jazz Festival, featuring

world-class performances by renowned jazz musicians. The Toronto International Film Festival (TIFF) in September attracts film enthusiasts and celebrities from around the world.

During the summer months, don't miss Caribana, a colorful celebration of Caribbean culture with vibrant parades, music, and delicious Caribbean cuisine. The Pride Parade in June is one of the largest LGBTQ+ events in North America, showcasing Toronto's inclusivity and diversity.

Top Attractions

Welcome to Toronto, the bustling metropolis and cultural hub of Canada! As the largest city in the country, Toronto offers a diverse array of attractions and experiences that captivate the hearts of locals and visitors alike. With its impressive skyline, multicultural neighborhoods, and vibrant arts scene, Toronto promises an unforgettable journey through its streets. In this Canada travel guide, we will delve into the top attractions that define the charm and allure of this remarkable city. From iconic landmarks to hidden gems, Toronto has something for everyone.

CN Tower :

Our exploration begins with the iconic CN Tower, a symbol of Toronto's skyline and one of the most recognized landmarks in Canada. Standing at a height of 553 meters, this engineering marvel offers breathtaking panoramic views of the city from its observation decks. Adventure-seekers can try the EdgeWalk, a thrilling hands-free walk around the tower's edge, or take the SkyPod elevator to the highest point for an even more awe-inspiring vista. The CN Tower also houses world-class dining options, including the revolving 360 Restaurant, where visitors can savor delicious cuisine while enjoying stunning vistas.

Royal Ontario Museum :

A treasure trove of art, culture, and natural history, the Royal Ontario Museum (ROM) is a must-visit attraction for travelers of all interests. With its distinctive architecture and extensive collection, the ROM offers an immersive journey through time and space. From dinosaur fossils to ancient artifacts, indigenous art to contemporary exhibitions, the museum showcases a wide range of captivating displays. Visitors can also participate in interactive exhibits, join guided tours, or attend lectures and workshops to enhance their understanding of the exhibits.

Distillery District :
For a taste of Toronto's rich history and vibrant arts scene, a visit to the Distillery District is essential. Located in a beautifully preserved Victorian industrial site, this pedestrian-only neighborhood features cobblestone streets, art galleries, boutiques, and numerous dining options. The Distillery District is renowned for its art installations, live performances, and cultural events throughout the year. Visitors can explore the distilleries that once produced whiskey and learn about their fascinating history, or simply stroll through the charming streets, admiring the unique blend of heritage and creativity.

Toronto Islands :
Escape the urban hustle and bustle by taking a short ferry ride to the Toronto Islands, a tranquil oasis just off the city's coast. Comprising a chain of small islands, this natural retreat offers a perfect respite from the city's energy. With its sandy beaches, scenic bike paths, and picnic areas, the

Toronto Islands are a favorite destination for outdoor enthusiasts and families. Visitors can rent bicycles, kayaks, or paddleboards to explore the islands' nooks and crannies, or simply relax on the shores and enjoy the stunning views of Toronto's skyline.

Art Gallery of Ontario:

Art aficionados will find their haven in the Art Gallery of Ontario (AGO), one of the largest art museums in North America. Housing an extensive collection spanning from ancient times to contemporary art, the AGO boasts works by renowned artists such as Rembrandt, Monet, and van Gogh. The museum's iconic architecture, including the iconic spiral staircase, adds to the allure of the space. In addition to its permanent collection, the AGO hosts various temporary exhibitions, art workshops, and interactive installations, providing a dynamic and immersive experience for visitors of all ages.

Dining and Nightlife

Toronto, the cosmopolitan capital of Ontario, is a city renowned for its diverse culture, world-class cuisine, and thriving nightlife. With a rich tapestry of culinary delights and an energetic after-hours scene, Toronto offers a memorable experience for travelers seeking exceptional dining and unforgettable nights out. In this travel guide, we will explore the multifaceted dining options and vibrant nightlife that Toronto has to offer, ensuring an immersive and enjoyable experience for visitors.

I. Dining in Toronto:

International Culinary Melting Pot:
Toronto boasts a culinary landscape that represents the city's multicultural fabric. Visitors can embark on a gastronomic journey exploring a wide range of international cuisines, from Chinese dim sum in Chinatown to vibrant Indian curries in Little India. Additionally, neighborhoods like Little Italy, Greektown, and Kensington Market offer authentic Italian, Greek, and global street food experiences, respectively.

Fine Dining Experiences:
For those seeking refined culinary experiences, Toronto is home to a plethora of fine dining establishments. The city showcases a blend of local and international flavors, as talented chefs fuse traditional techniques with innovative twists. Renowned restaurants like Canoe, Alo, and

Scaramouche offer impeccable service, breathtaking views, and exceptional cuisine, making them must-visit destinations for food enthusiasts.

Farm-to-Table and Locally Sourced Delights: Toronto's commitment to sustainable and locally sourced ingredients has given rise to a vibrant farm-to-table movement. Restaurants like Actinolite, Richmond Station, and Ruby Watchco emphasize seasonal produce, supporting local farmers and highlighting the region's natural bounty. Visitors can savor dishes prepared with fresh, organic ingredients, often showcased in tasting menus that embody the essence of Toronto's culinary philosophy.

Neighborhood Gems:
Exploring Toronto's diverse neighborhoods unveils hidden culinary gems waiting to be discovered. Stroll along Queen Street West to find trendy eateries, cozy cafes, and charming patisseries. The St. Lawrence Market offers a bustling atmosphere and a wide array of vendors selling fresh produce, artisanal cheeses, and international delicacies. Exploring the Danforth, known as Greektown, presents visitors with authentic Greek tavernas and lively patios during the summer months.

II. Toronto Nightlife:

Entertainment District:
Toronto's Entertainment District is the epicenter of the city's nightlife. King Street West, in particular, pulsates with energy as it houses a myriad of nightclubs, bars, and lounges. Visitors can revel in the vibrant atmosphere, hopping from one venue to another, enjoying live music, DJs, and performances that cater to a variety of tastes and genres.

Live Music Scene:
Toronto has a vibrant live music scene, with numerous venues showcasing local talent as well as international acts. The iconic Massey Hall, the Danforth Music Hall, and the Horseshoe Tavern are just a few venues that have played a significant role in the city's music culture. From indie bands to jazz ensembles, there is always a performance to suit every musical preference.

Craft Breweries and Distilleries:
Craft beer and spirits have gained significant popularity in recent years, and Toronto has embraced the trend wholeheartedly. The city is

home to a plethora of breweries and distilleries, offering unique and innovative libations. Visitors can embark on brewery tours, tasting sessions, and even attend beer festivals to explore the local craft beer scene and appreciate the art of brewing.

Unique Nighttime Experiences:
Toronto offers distinctive nighttime experiences beyond traditional bars and clubs. The city's vibrant theater scene allows visitors to catch a Broadway-quality show at the Royal Alexandra Theatre or enjoy a comedic performance at the Second City. Alternatively, one can marvel at the city's breathtaking skyline from a rooftop bar or embark on a nighttime cruise along Lake Ontario, combining stunning views with entertainment.

Shopping

Toronto, the cosmopolitan gem of Canada, is a thriving metropolis known for its diverse culture, stunning architecture, and a myriad of attractions. Among its many facets, the city boasts a remarkable shopping scene that caters to every taste and budget. From luxury boutiques to quirky vintage stores and bustling markets, Toronto offers an unparalleled shopping experience for visitors. In this Canada travel guide, we delve into the world of shopping in Toronto, highlighting the city's premier shopping districts, iconic malls, unique boutiques, and vibrant markets.

Shopping Districts:

Toronto is home to several distinct shopping districts, each with its own character and appeal. Here are some of the city's top shopping destinations:

a. Yorkville:

Nestled in the heart of downtown Toronto, Yorkville is renowned as the city's luxury shopping district. Here, you'll find high-end fashion boutiques, upscale brands, and designer labels. Luxury flagship stores such as Holt Renfrew and high-end international brands like Chanel and Prada grace the streets of this upscale neighborhood, offering a luxurious shopping experience.

b. Queen Street West:

Regarded as one of the coolest neighborhoods in the world, Queen Street West is a haven for independent boutiques, local designers, and trendy shops. Here, you can explore an array of unique fashion boutiques, art galleries, vintage shops, and stylish concept stores. The district is perfect for fashion enthusiasts seeking one-of-a-kind finds and cutting-edge designs.

c. Kensington Market:
For a more eclectic and bohemian shopping experience, head to Kensington Market. This vibrant neighborhood is bursting with character, offering a mix of vintage shops, thrift stores, independent retailers, and multicultural markets. It's an ideal place to discover vintage fashion, antiques, handmade crafts, and international delicacies.

d. Toronto Eaton Centre:
Located in the heart of downtown, the Toronto Eaton Centre is one of Canada's premier shopping destinations. With over 250 stores, including major international brands, this iconic mall is a shopaholic's paradise. Its stunning architecture, glass ceiling, and multi-level shopping experience make it a must-visit spot for both locals and tourists.

Unique Boutiques and Concept Stores:
Toronto is renowned for its thriving independent retail scene, boasting numerous unique boutiques and concept stores that offer curated selections of clothing, accessories, home decor, and more. Some notable boutiques include:

a. Drake General Store:
A beloved Toronto brand, the Drake General Store offers an eclectic mix of clothing, accessories, homeware, and gift items. With its focus on Canadian-made products, this store captures the essence of Toronto's creative spirit.

b. Coal Miner's Daughter:
Specializing in locally made clothing and accessories, Coal Miner's Daughter showcases the talents of Canadian designers. Its carefully curated collection of stylish and sustainable fashion pieces makes it a go-to destination for fashion-forward shoppers.

c. Likely General:
Located in the heart of the vibrant neighborhood of Roncesvalles, Likely General is a concept store that combines a curated boutique with an art gallery. It features an ever-changing selection of handmade goods, art, books, and unique gifts.

Vibrant Markets:
Toronto's markets offer an authentic and lively shopping experience. Here are a few noteworthy markets to explore:

a. St. Lawrence Market:
A historic Toronto landmark, St. Lawrence Market is a bustling market that has been serving the city since 1803. It houses a rich array of fresh produce, artisanal cheeses, baked goods, meats, and international delicacies. Take a leisurely stroll through its vibrant aisles, and immerse yourself in the city's culinary culture.

b. Kensington Market:
While mentioned earlier as a shopping district, Kensington Market is also a vibrant open-air market. Here, you'll find an assortment of food stalls, vintage shops, international spices, and unique handmade crafts. The market is a kaleidoscope of sights, sounds, and flavors, offering an immersive experience.

Cultural and Ethnic Shopping:
Toronto's diverse population has contributed to the emergence of various cultural shopping hubs, where you can explore ethnic markets, clothing

stores, and specialty shops. Some notable areas include:

a. Chinatown:

Toronto's Chinatown, centered around Spadina Avenue and Dundas Street, is a vibrant neighborhood brimming with shops, restaurants, and markets. Delight in authentic Asian cuisine, browse Chinese herbal medicine stores, and peruse traditional Chinese clothing boutiques.

b. Little Italy:

Stretching along College Street, Little Italy showcases Italian culture and heritage through its charming cafes, gelato shops, and specialty stores. It's the perfect place to pick up Italian delicacies, wines, and imported fashion items.

•*Vancouver*

Vancouver, located on the southwestern coast of British Columbia, is a vibrant and picturesque city that stands as a testament to the natural beauty of Canada. With its stunning landscapes, multicultural atmosphere, and thriving urban scene, Vancouver is a must-visit destination for travelers from around the world. In this comprehensive travel guide, we will explore the various facets of Vancouver, including its diverse neighborhoods, iconic attractions, outdoor adventures, culinary delights, and cultural offerings. Whether you are seeking breathtaking views of the mountains, exploring eclectic markets, or immersing yourself in world-class museums, Vancouver offers a wealth of experiences to suit every traveler's interests.

Neighborhoods and Landmarks

Vancouver is a city of distinct neighborhoods, each with its own charm and character. From the historic streets of Gastown to the trendy boutiques of Yaletown, there is something for everyone. Granville Island, a vibrant hub of art and culture, is a must-visit destination. Here, visitors can explore the public market, browse local artwork, and enjoy live performances at the Granville Island Theatre. For stunning views of the city, a visit to Stanley Park is essential. This sprawling urban oasis is home to lush forests, picturesque beaches, and the famous seawall, a scenic pathway that encircles the park and offers breathtaking vistas of the city skyline.

Outdoor Adventures

Nature enthusiasts will find an abundance of outdoor activities in and around Vancouver. Grouse Mountain, located just outside the city, offers year-round adventure with hiking trails, ziplining, and skiing in the winter months. The Capilano Suspension Bridge, a thrilling attraction that spans a lush canyon, provides an opportunity to immerse yourself in the beauty of the temperate rainforest. For a day trip, consider visiting Whistler, a world-renowned ski resort known for its superb slopes and stunning alpine scenery. Additionally, the nearby North Shore Mountains offer opportunities for hiking, mountain biking, and breathtaking panoramic views.

Culinary Delights

Vancouver's culinary scene is a delightful fusion of flavors from around the world. The city's multicultural makeup is reflected in its diverse array of dining options. From fresh seafood on Granville Island to Asian-inspired cuisine in the vibrant neighborhoods of Chinatown and Richmond, Vancouver offers a gastronomic adventure like no other. For a taste of local delicacies, don't miss the chance to try poutine, a Canadian classic consisting of French fries smothered in cheese curds and gravy. The city is also known for its thriving craft beer scene, with numerous breweries offering tastings and tours for beer enthusiasts.

Cultural Offerings

Vancouver boasts a rich cultural tapestry, with a plethora of museums, galleries, and performing arts venues. The Museum of Anthropology at the University of British Columbia showcases indigenous art and artifacts, providing insight into the diverse First Nations cultures of the region. The Vancouver Art Gallery is home to an impressive collection of contemporary and historical art, while the Science World offers interactive exhibits that appeal to visitors of all ages. The city also hosts a variety of festivals throughout the year, such as the Vancouver International Jazz Festival and the Celebration of Light fireworks competition, adding vibrancy and excitement to the cultural calendar.

Day Trips and Excursions

Beyond the city limits, Vancouver serves as a gateway to a host of memorable day trips. A visit to Victoria, the capital of British Columbia, is a popular choice, with its charming harbor, historic architecture, and the renowned Butchart Gardens. The Sea-to-Sky Highway offers a scenic drive to the town of Squamish, where adventure seekers can enjoy activities like rock climbing and kiteboarding. For a taste of the Canadian wilderness, consider a trip to the Gulf Islands, a picturesque archipelago known for its idyllic beaches, quaint villages, and abundant wildlife.

Top Attractions

Nestled between the Pacific Ocean and the Coastal Mountains, Vancouver stands as a vibrant and diverse metropolis on Canada's West Coast. Boasting a harmonious blend of breathtaking natural landscapes, a thriving cultural scene, and a remarkable culinary landscape, this coastal city offers an unparalleled experience to its visitors. As a prominent destination in Canada, Vancouver is renowned for its majestic mountains, stunning waterfront, and lush parks. In this comprehensive travel guide, we will delve into the top attractions that make Vancouver an irresistible destination for travelers seeking a perfect blend of urban adventures and outdoor escapes.

Stanley Park: Nature's Paradise in the Heart of the City :

Begin your journey in Vancouver by immersing yourself in the pristine beauty of Stanley Park. As one of the largest urban parks in North America, this verdant oasis stretches over 1,000 acres and offers a myriad of activities for all ages. Explore the park's lush trails, rent a bike to circumnavigate the seawall, or embark on a horse-drawn carriage ride to admire the breathtaking views of the mountains and the sparkling waters of the Burrard Inlet. Don't miss visiting the Vancouver Aquarium, nestled within Stanley Park, which showcases a diverse array of marine life.

Granville Island: A Feast for the Senses :

Located just a stone's throw away from downtown Vancouver, Granville Island is a bustling hub of culture, art, and gastronomy. Discover the Granville Island Public Market, a food lover's paradise where local artisans and farmers showcase their fresh produce, delectable baked goods, and unique culinary creations. Wander through the vibrant art galleries, boutique shops, and theaters that make Granville Island an artistic haven. Take a leisurely stroll along the waterfront, where you can witness talented street performers and enjoy breathtaking views of the city skyline.

Grouse Mountain: A Natural Wonderland:
Rising majestically above Vancouver's skyline, Grouse Mountain offers an unforgettable alpine experience throughout the year. In winter, thrill-seekers can hit the slopes for skiing and snowboarding, while summer visitors can embark on scenic hikes amidst the picturesque trails. Take a ride on the Skyride, a gondola that offers panoramic views of the city, or witness the mesmerizing Lumberjack Show, showcasing the region's rich logging history. Don't forget to meet the resident grizzly bears at the wildlife refuge and visit the Eye of the Wind, a wind turbine with an observation deck that provides awe-inspiring vistas of the surrounding landscapes.

Capilano Suspension Bridge Park: A Thrilling Treetop Adventure :
Indulge your sense of adventure at the Capilano Suspension Bridge Park, an iconic Vancouver attraction that offers a thrilling experience amidst the coastal rainforest. Traverse the suspension bridge, suspended 230 feet above the Capilano River, and feel the exhilaration as you walk amidst

the towering trees. Explore the Treetops Adventure, a series of suspended walkways that offer a unique perspective of the lush canopy. Additionally, the park features the Cliffwalk, a cantilevered walkway clinging to the granite cliffs, providing breathtaking views of the surrounding canyon.

Museum of Anthropology: Immersive Cultural Exploration :

Delve into the rich indigenous history and artistry of the Pacific Northwest at the Museum of Anthropology, located at the University of British Columbia. The museum showcases a vast collection of artifacts, including intricate First Nations totem poles, historical objects, and contemporary indigenous art. Gain insight into the cultural traditions, beliefs, and stories of the region's indigenous peoples through engaging exhibitions and immersive displays. The stunning architecture of the museum, designed by renowned architect Arthur Erickson, is an attraction in itself.

Dining and Nightlife

Nestled on the stunning Pacific coast, Vancouver, Canada's bustling metropolis, offers a diverse and vibrant culinary and nightlife scene that caters to a wide range of tastes and preferences. This comprehensive travel guide explores the city's exceptional dining options, from exquisite seafood to global cuisines, and delves into the captivating nightlife that awaits visitors after sunset. Join us as we embark on a culinary and nocturnal journey through the enchanting city of Vancouver.

I. Dining in Vancouver:

Pacific Northwest Delicacies:

Seafood Galore: Vancouver's coastal location makes it a haven for fresh and delectable seafood. Sample succulent Dungeness crab, spot prawns, and wild Pacific salmon at renowned seafood restaurants like Blue Water Cafe and Joe Fortes Seafood & Chop House.
West Coast Cuisine: Embrace the flavors of the Pacific Northwest with dishes that emphasize local ingredients, such as foraged mushrooms, wild berries, and organic produce. Restaurants like Hawksworth and Farmer's Apprentice showcase the region's culinary prowess.

Indigenous Fare: Explore the indigenous culinary traditions of the First Nations people through establishments like Salmon n' Bannock, offering unique dishes like cedar-plank salmon and bison stew.

International Flavors:

Asian Fusion: Vancouver boasts a vibrant Asian community, resulting in an abundance of exceptional Asian fusion restaurants. Delight in the flavors of Chinese, Japanese, Vietnamese, and Thai cuisines, with favorites like Bao Bei, Miku, and Phnom Penh.

Global Gastronomy: The city's diverse population has fostered a multicultural culinary scene. Savor flavors from around the world at renowned eateries like Vij's (Indian), La Quercia (Italian), and Medina Cafe (Mediterranean-inspired brunch).

Food Markets and Food Trucks:

Granville Island Public Market: Wander through this iconic market, offering an array of fresh produce, artisanal cheeses, baked goods, and more. Enjoy a casual lunch from the market's food stalls, featuring options like gourmet grilled cheese sandwiches and freshly shucked oysters.

Food Truck Culture: Vancouver's streets come alive with an impressive assortment of food trucks, offering diverse and delicious street eats. From gourmet burgers to inventive tacos, these mobile kitchens provide quick and flavorsome meals at reasonable prices.

II. Vancouver's Lively Nightlife:

Gastown:

Historic Charm: Discover Vancouver's oldest neighborhood, Gastown, which blends cobblestone streets with trendy bars, pubs, and clubs. Take in the iconic Gastown Steam Clock and explore establishments like The Diamond and Guilt & Company for craft cocktails and live music. Speakeasy Vibe: Unleash your inner adventurer and venture into hidden speakeasies, such as Prohibition and The Keefer Bar, where mixologists craft innovative and tantalizing concoctions. Yaletown:

Upscale Atmosphere: Yaletown offers a sophisticated nightlife experience, with its converted warehouses turned upscale bars, lounges, and clubs. Enjoy a refined evening at Bar None or

The Opus Bar, known for their stylish ambiance and top-notch cocktails.
Granville Street:

Entertainment District: Granville Street is the heart of Vancouver's entertainment scene, teeming with clubs, live music venues, and vibrant dance floors. Embrace the electric energy at venues like Venue Nightclub and Commodore Ballroom, hosting renowned musicians and DJs.
Craft Breweries:

Craft Beer Revolution: Vancouver has embraced the craft beer movement, offering a plethora of breweries and tasting rooms. Experience the local brews at places like Brassneck Brewery, Parallel 49 Brewing, and Steamworks Brewing Company.

Outdoor Activities

Vancouver, located on the picturesque west coast of Canada, offers a wide array of outdoor activities for adventure enthusiasts and nature lovers alike. With its stunning natural landscapes, mild climate, and proximity to mountains, forests, and the Pacific Ocean, Vancouver is a haven for outdoor exploration. Whether you enjoy hiking, biking, water sports, or simply immersing yourself in the beauty of nature, Vancouver has something to offer for everyone.

Stanley Park: A must-visit destination in Vancouver, Stanley Park is a sprawling urban park that spans over 400 hectares. This park offers numerous outdoor activities, including scenic walking and biking trails that wind through lush forests, along the seawall, and around the park's famous seawater pool, Second Beach. You can also rent a bike or rollerblades to explore the park at your own pace.

Grouse Mountain: Just a short drive from downtown Vancouver, Grouse Mountain is a popular destination for outdoor enthusiasts. In the summer, you can take the Skyride gondola to the mountaintop, where you'll find hiking trails offering breathtaking views of the city and surrounding landscapes. For thrill-seekers, there are opportunities for zip-lining and paragliding. In winter, Grouse Mountain transforms into a winter wonderland, offering skiing, snowboarding, and snowshoeing.

Capilano Suspension Bridge Park: This iconic attraction is located in the North Shore of Vancouver. The highlight of the park is the suspension bridge that hangs 70 meters above the Capilano River, providing a thrilling experience and stunning views of the lush rainforest below. The park also offers treetop walkways, cliffside trails, and a rainforest ecology center, providing a unique opportunity to learn about the local flora and fauna.

Whistler: Known for its world-class ski resorts, Whistler is a scenic two-hour drive from Vancouver. In addition to skiing and snowboarding during the winter months, Whistler also offers a host of outdoor activities during the summer. You can explore the vast network of hiking and mountain biking trails, go zip-lining, golfing, or enjoy water activities such as kayaking or paddleboarding on the nearby lakes.

Kayaking in False Creek: Vancouver's downtown waterfront is perfect for a leisurely kayak tour. Paddle along False Creek, taking in the stunning skyline views, passing under bridges, and enjoying the lively atmosphere. You can also venture further to explore the nearby Granville Island, where you can find a vibrant public market and eclectic shops.

Lynn Canyon Park: For a nature escape within the city, Lynn Canyon Park offers beautiful trails, a suspension bridge, and breathtaking waterfalls. Hike through the dense forest, cool off in the swimming holes, or capture stunning photos of the Lynn Canyon Suspension Bridge, a free alternative to the nearby Capilano Suspension Bridge.

Beaches: Vancouver boasts several stunning beaches along its coastline, where you can relax, soak up the sun, and enjoy various water activities. English Bay Beach, Kitsilano Beach, and Spanish Banks are popular choices for beachgoers. You can rent paddleboards or kayaks, go for a swim, or simply enjoy a picnic while enjoying the magnificent mountain and ocean views.

These are just a few examples of the numerous outdoor activities available in Vancouver. The city's natural beauty, coupled with its commitment to preserving green spaces, makes it an ideal destination for those seeking to immerse themselves in nature and enjoy the great outdoors. Whether you're an adrenaline junkie or prefer a more leisurely experience, Vancouver has something to offer for every type of traveler.

•*Montreal*

Montreal, the cultural capital of Canada, is a city that seamlessly blends old-world charm with a modern cosmopolitan vibe. Situated in the province of Quebec, Montreal stands as a testament to Canada's cultural diversity, with a unique fusion of French and English influences. This dynamic metropolis offers visitors a myriad of experiences, from its historic architecture and world-class museums to its vibrant festivals and delectable culinary scene. In this comprehensive travel guide, we will delve into the various facets of Montreal, highlighting its must-visit attractions, iconic landmarks, cultural events, and culinary delights, ensuring an unforgettable journey for all travelers.

Historical and Architectural Marvels :
Montreal's rich history is palpable in its captivating architecture and preserved landmarks. Begin your exploration in Old Montreal, the city's historic heart, where cobblestone streets lead you past beautifully restored buildings. Discover the iconic Notre-Dame Basilica, a masterpiece of Gothic Revival architecture with its stunning interior adorned with intricate woodwork and vibrant stained glass windows.
The historic district is also home to Place Jacques-Cartier, a lively square teeming with street performers, cafes, and boutiques. Nearby, the Bonsecours Market showcases exquisite craftsmanship and local artisanal products.

Montreal's architectural wonders extend beyond Old Montreal. The Habitat 67 complex, designed by renowned architect Moshe Safdie, is a must-see.

This innovative housing complex features a unique arrangement of stacked cubes, creating a visually striking landmark.

For a panoramic view of the city, visit Mount Royal, a hill at the heart of Montreal. Ascend to the belvedere and marvel at the breathtaking vista of the city skyline, St. Lawrence River, and surrounding green spaces.

Cultural Delights and Museums :
Montreal embraces culture in all its forms, offering an array of world-class museums and artistic experiences. The Montreal Museum of Fine Arts boasts an impressive collection spanning centuries, with works by renowned artists such as Picasso, Rembrandt, and Van Gogh. The museum also hosts captivating temporary exhibitions that showcase contemporary art and emerging talents.
Immerse yourself in Montreal's vibrant music scene by attending a concert at the iconic Place des Arts. This cultural complex is home to multiple performance venues, including the renowned Montreal Symphony House. From classical concerts to Broadway shows and international music festivals, there is something for every taste.

To delve into Montreal's rich history and heritage, visit the Pointe-à-Callière Museum. Located on the very spot where Montreal was founded, this museum offers captivating exhibits that showcase the city's archaeological treasures and chronicle its evolution.

Festivals and Celebrations :
Montreal is renowned for its lively festivals that celebrate music, arts, and cultural diversity. The Montreal International Jazz Festival, the largest of its kind in the world, takes over the city every summer. Enjoy free outdoor concerts, intimate performances in jazz clubs, and electrifying street festivities.

Another highlight is the Just for Laughs Festival, where renowned comedians gather to entertain audiences with their wit and humor. Be prepared for laughter-filled evenings and unexpected encounters with street performers throughout the city.

During the warmer months, the Montreal International Fireworks Competition lights up the night sky with breathtaking pyrotechnic displays. The competition attracts participants from around the globe, transforming Montreal into a dazzling spectacle of colors and lights.

Gastronomic Delights :
Montreal's culinary scene is a melting pot of flavors, offering a wide range of international cuisines alongside iconic local specialties. Indulge in poutine, a quintessential Canadian dish consisting of crispy fries topped with cheese curds and smothered in rich gravy. For an elevated culinary experience, explore the city's diverse neighborhoods and sample dishes from renowned chefs.
Head to Little Italy to savor authentic Italian flavors, from mouthwatering pizzas to homemade pasta. In the Mile End district, try Montreal-style bagels, baked in wood-fired ovens and known for their distinctive sweetness and chewiness.

Exploring the city's vibrant food markets, such as Jean-Talon Market and Atwater Market, is a treat for the senses. These bustling hubs offer fresh produce, local delicacies, and international ingredients, making them the perfect place to indulge in gastronomic delights.

Outdoor Recreation and Nature Escapes :

While Montreal is a bustling urban center, it also provides ample opportunities for outdoor activities and nature escapes. The extensive network of parks and green spaces invites locals and visitors alike to enjoy picnics, cycling, and leisurely strolls. Parc du Mont-Royal, with its vast trails and stunning vistas, is a haven for outdoor enthusiasts.

In winter, embrace the Canadian spirit and try ice skating in one of Montreal's outdoor rinks, such as the iconic Bonsecours Basin or the Natrel Skating Rink in the Old Port. The city also offers cross-country skiing and snowshoeing options in its beautiful parks.

For a day trip outside the city, explore the stunning Laurentian Mountains. Just a short drive away, these picturesque mountains offer hiking, skiing, and other outdoor activities, providing a refreshing escape from the urban hustle and bustle.

Top Attractions

Nestled in the heart of the Canadian province of Quebec, Montreal is a captivating city that seamlessly blends history, culture, and modernity.

With its picturesque streets, stunning architecture, and a rich tapestry of diverse communities, Montreal offers an unparalleled experience for travelers seeking a unique and immersive journey. In this travel guide, we will delve into the top attractions that make Montreal a must-visit destination, from its historic landmarks to its vibrant cultural scene.

Old Montreal:
A journey through Montreal would be incomplete without a visit to the historic heart of the city, Old Montreal. This charming district showcases a remarkable fusion of old-world European charm and North American influence. Explore the cobbled streets lined with beautifully preserved buildings, such as the iconic Notre-Dame Basilica, a stunning example of Gothic Revival architecture. Immerse yourself in history at Pointe-à-Callière, the birthplace of Montreal, where you can delve into the city's rich heritage through interactive exhibits.

Mount Royal:
Rising majestically above the city, Mount Royal is an oasis of tranquility and natural beauty. Embark on a hike or leisurely stroll through Mount Royal Park, designed by the same landscape architect as

New York City's Central Park. Enjoy panoramic views of the city skyline, picnic by the serene Lac des Castors (Beaver Lake), and visit the iconic Mount Royal Chalet. This iconic landmark provides breathtaking views of Montreal and is a prime location to witness the sunset painting the city in warm hues.

The Underground City:
Escape the hustle and bustle of the city streets and explore Montreal's unique Underground City, a vast network of interconnected tunnels and shopping complexes. With over 20 miles of tunnels, this subterranean world offers a respite from cold winters and hosts a plethora of shopping centers, restaurants, museums, and even theaters. Don't miss the remarkable architecture of the Palais des congrès and the contemporary art installations throughout the underground galleries.

The Plateau-Mont-Royal:
The Plateau-Mont-Royal neighborhood is a vibrant and trendy area that captures the essence of Montreal's artistic and bohemian spirit. Wander along the colorful streets lined with charming Victorian houses, browse through eclectic boutiques, and savor a diverse culinary scene. Visit

the iconic Saint-Laurent Boulevard, known as "The Main," which has been the heart of Montreal's cultural scene for decades, featuring art galleries, live music venues, and trendy bars.

Montreal Museum of Fine Arts:
Art enthusiasts will be delighted by the Montreal Museum of Fine Arts, one of the city's premier cultural institutions. With a collection spanning centuries and continents, the museum showcases an impressive array of art, including paintings, sculptures, decorative arts, and contemporary works. Don't miss the museum's permanent collection, featuring artists like Rembrandt, Picasso, and Warhol, or the rotating exhibitions that highlight both local and international talent.

Jean-Talon Market:
For a true sensory experience, head to the Jean-Talon Market, North America's largest open-air market. Located in the Little Italy district, this bustling marketplace offers an abundance of fresh produce, local delicacies, artisanal products, and vibrant flowers. Immerse yourself in the sights, sounds, and scents as you stroll through the stalls, interact with local vendors, and indulge in culinary

delights, including Quebecois specialties like poutine and maple syrup treats.

Saint Joseph's Oratory:

A beacon of spirituality and architectural grandeur, Saint Joseph's Oratory is a must-visit attraction in Montreal. This awe-inspiring basilica is dedicated to Saint Joseph, the patron saint of Canada, and is renowned for its stunning dome, intricate mosaics, and peaceful gardens. Climb the steps to reach the top of the Oratory and enjoy panoramic views of the city, or spend a reflective moment in the serene ambiance of the Crypt Church.

Quartier des Spectacles:

Montreal's Quartier des Spectacles is a vibrant cultural hub that comes alive with festivals, concerts, and artistic performances throughout the year. This lively district boasts numerous theaters, performance venues, and public spaces, creating a dynamic atmosphere for visitors to immerse themselves in the city's thriving arts scene. Don't miss the renowned Montreal International Jazz Festival, the Just for Laughs comedy festival, or the immersive multimedia installations of the annual Luminothérapie event.

Cultural Experiences

Montreal, the largest city in the province of Quebec, is a captivating destination that seamlessly blends European charm with North American allure. This bustling metropolis is renowned for its rich history, diverse population, and vibrant cultural scene. In this comprehensive Canada travel guide, we will delve into the fascinating cultural experiences that await you in Montreal, offering insights into its iconic landmarks, festivals, culinary delights, and artistic heritage. From the cobblestone streets of Old Montreal to the contemporary art galleries of the Plateau-Mont-Royal district, get ready to immerse yourself in the dynamic cultural tapestry of this captivating city.

Old Montreal: (Stepping into the Past)

Begin your journey in Montreal by exploring the historic heart of the city, Old Montreal. As you stroll through the cobblestone streets, you'll be transported back in time to the city's colonial era. Marvel at the stunning architecture, such as the Notre-Dame Basilica with its Gothic Revival style, and the majestic Bonsecours Market, a former city hall turned vibrant marketplace. Take a guided walking tour to learn about the area's history and visit Pointe-à-Callière, a renowned archaeology museum that showcases Montreal's intriguing past. The Place Jacques-Cartier square is a vibrant hub where street performers entertain visitors, and local restaurants offer a taste of traditional Quebecois cuisine.

Museums and Art Galleries:(A Haven for Culture Enthusiasts)

Montreal boasts a wealth of museums and art galleries that cater to a wide range of interests. The Montreal Museum of Fine Arts is a must-visit, housing an extensive collection spanning centuries and continents. The contemporary art scene thrives at the Montreal Museum of Contemporary Art (MAC), showcasing innovative works from both local and international artists. History buffs will appreciate the McCord Museum, which chronicles the social history of Montreal, and the Biosphere, an interactive museum dedicated to environmental sustainability. To dive deeper into Montreal's artistic heritage, explore the Plateau-Mont-Royal district, home to numerous independent galleries and artist studios.

Festivals and Celebrations:)A Year-Round Extravaganza)

Montreal is renowned for its vibrant festival scene, offering a year-round extravaganza of music, art, and cultural celebrations. The Montreal International Jazz Festival is one of the world's largest jazz festivals, attracting top musicians from around the globe. The Just for Laughs Festival brings laughter to the streets with its renowned comedy shows. During the summer, the Montreal International Fireworks Competition illuminates the night sky with mesmerizing pyrotechnic displays. The Montreal International Documentary Festival (RIDM), the Montreal Fringe Festival, and the Nuit Blanche are just a few of the many events that showcase the city's creative spirit.

Cuisine:(A Gastronomic Adventure)

No visit to Montreal is complete without indulging in its diverse and delectable culinary offerings. Begin your gastronomic adventure with a visit to Schwartz's Deli, an iconic establishment known for its mouthwatering smoked meat sandwiches. Immerse yourself in the flavors of the city's thriving food scene by exploring the diverse neighborhoods, such as the Mile End and Little Italy, which offer a wide array of international cuisines. Sample poutine, a quintessential Canadian dish of crispy fries smothered in cheese curds and gravy, and indulge in maple syrup treats. Don't forget to experience Montreal's vibrant café culture, with cozy spots that serve delicious coffee and pastries.

Multicultural Neighborhoods:(Exploring the Diversity)

Montreal's cultural mosaic is reflected in its diverse neighborhoods. Stroll through Chinatown, where you can savor authentic Asian cuisine and browse vibrant markets. Visit Little Italy, where you can enjoy mouthwatering Italian delicacies and explore the Jean-Talon Market, a paradise for food lovers. The Plateau-Mont-Royal district is known for its bohemian atmosphere, charming streets, and artistic vibe. This neighborhood is a treasure trove of unique boutiques, art galleries, and cozy cafes. Le Village, the city's LGBTQ+ district, is a lively and inclusive area with a vibrant nightlife scene.

Festivals and Events

Montreal, the vibrant metropolis nestled in the province of Quebec, Canada, is renowned for its rich cultural heritage and dynamic events scene. The city proudly showcases a diverse array of festivals and events throughout the year, attracting locals and tourists alike. From celebrating music and film to embracing culinary delights and cultural traditions, Montreal offers a tapestry of experiences that captivate the senses. In this Canada travel guide, we delve into the captivating world of festivals and events in Montreal, exploring the city's most notable celebrations and highlighting the unique cultural tapestry that makes it a must-visit destination.

The Montreal International Jazz Festival:

Considered one of the most prestigious jazz festivals globally, the Montreal International Jazz Festival is a grand celebration of music, attracting over 2 million visitors annually. Spanning multiple stages throughout the city, this event showcases a diverse range of jazz, blues, and world music performances. Established in 1980, the festival has hosted world-renowned musicians, including legends like Ella Fitzgerald and Ray Charles. With both free and ticketed shows, music enthusiasts can immerse themselves in the soul-stirring melodies and rhythms that reverberate through the streets of Montreal.

Just for Laughs Festival:

Laughter takes center stage during the Just for Laughs Festival, a world-renowned comedy event that has been tickling funny bones since 1983. This annual extravaganza showcases a remarkable lineup of stand-up comedians, sketch troupes, and comedy galas. The festival attracts some of the biggest names in comedy, providing endless laughter for locals and visitors alike. From intimate performances in comedy clubs to large-scale outdoor shows, Just for Laughs guarantees an uproarious experience for all.

Montreal International Fireworks Competition:

Prepare to be dazzled by the Montreal International Fireworks Competition, a spectacular event that lights up the night sky with awe-inspiring pyrotechnic displays. Taking place over several summer weekends, this competition gathers the world's leading fireworks experts, who choreograph magnificent displays synchronized to music. Spectators gather along the waterfront to witness the sky explode with vibrant colors, creating a magical atmosphere that is nothing short of breathtaking.

Montreal Grand Prix:
Revving engines, high-speed thrills, and a vibrant atmosphere await motorsport enthusiasts at the Montreal Grand Prix. Held annually at the Circuit Gilles Villeneuve, this prestigious Formula One race draws crowds from around the globe. Alongside the thrilling on-track action, the city comes alive with festivities, parties, and exclusive events that celebrate the spirit of racing. Whether you're a die-hard racing fan or simply looking for a weekend filled with adrenaline, the Montreal Grand Prix is an event not to be missed.

Montreal International Documentary Festival (RIDM):
Film lovers are in for a treat at the Montreal International Documentary Festival, commonly known as RIDM. As Canada's largest documentary festival, RIDM showcases thought-provoking documentaries from around the world. From environmental issues to human rights and social justice, the festival explores a wide range of topics through compelling storytelling. Attendees have the opportunity to engage with filmmakers, participate

in panel discussions, and gain unique insights into the power of documentary cinema.

Montreal en Lumière:

Celebrating the arts, gastronomy, and winter magic, Montreal en Lumière is a captivating festival that brightens the city's winter months. The event combines culinary experiences, live performances, and outdoor activities, offering a vibrant fusion of culture and entertainment. Visitors can indulge in gourmet delights at the renowned gastronomy program, enjoy live music performances, and marvel at breathtaking light installations that illuminate the city's streets. Montreal en Lumière is a true celebration of creativity and winter enchantment.

International Balloon Festival of Saint-Jean-sur-Richelieu:

Just a short drive from Montreal, the International Balloon Festival of Saint-Jean-sur-Richelieu brings together hot air balloon enthusiasts from around the world. This multi-day event fills the skies with a colorful display of balloons, creating a mesmerizing spectacle for all ages. Alongside the balloon flights, visitors can enjoy live entertainment, amusement park rides, and various family-friendly activities.

The festival's joyful atmosphere and whimsical charm make it a delightful experience for both locals and travelers.

•Quebec City

Quebec City, the capital of the Canadian province of Quebec, is a captivating destination that seamlessly blends old-world charm with modern vibrancy. Steeped in rich history, boasting stunning architecture, and enveloped by breathtaking natural beauty, this UNESCO World Heritage Site is a must-visit for travelers seeking a unique and immersive experience. In this travel guide, we will delve into the fascinating facets of Quebec City, from its iconic landmarks and cultural treasures to its delectable cuisine and exciting festivals.

Historic District of Old Quebec:
The heart and soul of Quebec City lies within the Historic District of Old Quebec. Divided into two sections, the Upper Town (Haute-Ville) and Lower Town (Basse-Ville), this well-preserved area showcases a tapestry of cobblestone streets, fortified walls, and architectural marvels. Must-visit

sites include the iconic Château Frontenac, the Citadel, the historic Plains of Abraham, and the picturesque Quartier Petit Champlain, the oldest commercial district in North America.

Château Frontenac:
Perched high on a bluff overlooking the St. Lawrence River, the Château Frontenac is an emblematic landmark and an architectural masterpiece. Built in the late 19th century, this grand hotel exudes elegance and offers unparalleled views of the city. Visitors can explore its lavish interiors, enjoy a meal at one of its fine dining establishments, or simply soak in the atmosphere while strolling along the Dufferin Terrace.

Cultural Gems:
Quebec City boasts a thriving arts and culture scene, with a wealth of museums, galleries, and theaters to explore. The Musée de la Civilisation offers captivating exhibitions on Quebec's history, while the Musée National des Beaux-Arts showcases an impressive collection of Canadian and international art. Theater enthusiasts will delight in performances at the historic Théâtre Capitole or the vibrant Grand Théâtre de Québec.

Festivals and Events:

Throughout the year, Quebec City comes alive with a multitude of festivals and events that celebrate its unique heritage and lively spirit. The Winter Carnival, one of the world's largest winter festivals, transforms the city into a magical wonderland, complete with ice sculptures, parades, and outdoor activities. The New France Festival takes visitors back in time to the city's colonial era, while the Festival d'Été de Québec showcases renowned musicians from around the world.

Gastronomic Delights:

Quebec City is a culinary haven, offering a tantalizing array of gastronomic delights. From traditional Quebecois cuisine to international fare, the city's restaurants and cafes cater to all tastes. Indulge in poutine, a beloved Canadian dish of fries topped with cheese curds and gravy, or savor the flavors of maple syrup-infused dishes. Don't miss a visit to the Old Port Market (Marché du Vieux-Port) to sample local produce, artisanal cheeses, and freshly baked pastries.

Outdoor Adventures:

Nature lovers will find ample opportunities for outdoor exploration in and around Quebec City.

The Parc de la Chute-Montmorency, located just outside the city, is home to a spectacular waterfall that is higher than Niagara Falls. Visitors can hike the trails, take a cable car ride, or try ziplining for a thrilling experience. In the winter, nearby ski resorts such as Mont-Sainte-Anne and Stoneham offer excellent downhill skiing and snowboarding.

Day Trips:

Quebec City serves as a gateway to several enchanting day trip destinations. The charming Île d'Orléans, located just a short drive from the city, is known for its picturesque countryside, historic villages, and orchards. The Montmorency Falls Park and the Basilica of Sainte-Anne-de-Beaupré are other popular attractions within easy reach.

Top Attractions

Nestled on the banks of the majestic St. Lawrence River, Quebec City stands as a captivating destination that seamlessly blends old-world European charm with North American allure. As the capital of the province of Quebec, this historic city is renowned for its well-preserved colonial architecture, cobblestone streets, and a rich cultural heritage that dates back centuries. In this comprehensive travel guide, we will explore the top attractions that make Quebec City a must-visit destination for travelers seeking a blend of history, culture, and natural beauty.

I. Old Quebec and the Historic Districts

1.1. Vieux-Québec: Step into the pages of history as you wander through the UNESCO World Heritage-listed Vieux-Québec (Old Quebec). Divided into Upper Town (Haute-Ville) and Lower Town (Basse-Ville), this historic district is brimming with 17th-century architecture, fortified walls, and picturesque streets.

1.2. Place Royale: Located in the Lower Town, this vibrant square is the birthplace of French civilization in North America. Admire the beautiful Notre-Dame-des-Victoires Church and immerse yourself in the rich historical ambiance.

1.3. Quartier Petit Champlain: Explore one of North America's oldest commercial districts, known for its charming boutiques, art galleries, and quaint cafés. Stroll along Rue du Petit Champlain, a pedestrian-only street, and relish the unique atmosphere.

1.4. Plains of Abraham: Discover the site of the famous 1759 Battle of Quebec and enjoy the vast green expanse that now serves as a stunning urban park. Take a leisurely walk, have a picnic, or attend one of the many festivals held throughout the year.

II. Iconic Landmarks :

2.1. Château Frontenac: An architectural gem dominating the Quebec City skyline, the iconic Château Frontenac is a symbol of the city. Admire its stunning turrets and towers, indulge in a luxurious stay, or simply enjoy panoramic views of the river and cityscape from Dufferin Terrace.

2.2. Citadelle of Quebec: Explore the largest British fortress in North America and home to the prestigious Royal 22e Régiment. Witness the changing of the guard ceremony, visit the museum, and enjoy the magnificent views overlooking the St. Lawrence River.

2.3. Notre-Dame de Québec Basilica-Cathedral: Immerse yourself in the spiritual heart of Quebec City at this majestic cathedral. Marvel at its stunning architecture, intricate woodwork, and beautiful stained glass windows.

2.4. Parliament Hill: Located in the heart of the city, the Parliament Building showcases stunning neoclassical architecture. Join a guided tour to learn about the province's political history and explore the remarkable interior.

III. Cultural Experiences :

3.1. Musée de la Civilisation: Delve into Quebec's rich heritage through captivating exhibits, interactive displays, and multimedia presentations. This museum offers a fascinating exploration of Quebec's culture, history, and contemporary society.

3.2. Musée National des Beaux-Arts du Québec: Discover a vast collection of fine arts, sculptures, and decorative arts spanning from the 17th century to contemporary works. Explore the museum's permanent and temporary exhibitions that celebrate Quebec's artistic contributions.

3.3. Festival d'été de Québec: Join the largest outdoor music festival in Canada, held annually in July. Experience a diverse lineup of artists, including internationally acclaimed acts, spread across multiple stages in the heart of the city.

3.4. Rue Saint-Jean: Immerse yourself in the local vibe as you explore this lively street teeming with shops, restaurants, and bars. Savor delicious local cuisine, browse unique boutiques, and soak in the vibrant atmosphere.

IV. Natural Beauty and Outdoor Activities :

4.1. Montmorency Falls Park: Just a short drive from the city, witness the awe-inspiring

Montmorency Falls, which are taller than Niagara Falls. Take a cable car ride, cross the suspension bridge, or venture on hiking trails for breathtaking views.

4.2. Île d'Orléans: Embark on a scenic journey to this charming island known for its picturesque landscapes, quaint villages, and agricultural heritage. Explore the local farms, taste delectable regional produce, and soak in the tranquil ambiance.

4.3. Parc de la Chute-Montmorency: Admire the stunning Montmorency Falls from different vantage points in this scenic park. Enjoy outdoor activities such as ziplining, hiking, and biking while surrounded by the beauty of nature.

4.4. Biking along the St. Lawrence River: Rent a bike and embark on a memorable ride along the majestic St. Lawrence River. Follow the scenic bike paths that offer breathtaking views, picturesque neighborhoods, and idyllic picnic spots.

Historic Sites

Quebec City, nestled on the banks of the majestic St. Lawrence River, is a true testament to Canada's rich history and cultural heritage. With its cobblestone streets, charming architecture, and a captivating blend of French and North American influences, this enchanting city offers a glimpse into the past like no other. In this travel guide, we will embark on a remarkable journey through the historic sites of Quebec City, immersing ourselves in its captivating stories and experiencing the vibrant tapestry of its past.

Old Quebec :

Our exploration begins with the heart and soul of Quebec City - Old Quebec, a UNESCO World Heritage Site and the only fortified city north of Mexico. Divided into the Upper Town (Haute-Ville) and Lower Town (Basse-Ville), this historic district is a living museum, brimming with architectural marvels, fascinating museums, and bustling streets. a. Place Royale: Start your journey in Place Royale, the birthplace of French civilization in North America. Admire the charming square surrounded by 17th-century stone buildings, including the Notre-Dame-des-Victoires Church.

b. Château Frontenac: Dominating the city's skyline, the iconic Château Frontenac is a world-renowned luxury hotel and a symbol of

Quebec City. Marvel at its grandeur and panoramic views from Dufferin Terrace.

c. Citadelle of Quebec: Explore the star-shaped fortress, Citadelle of Quebec, the largest British-built fortress in North America. Witness the Changing of the Guard ceremony and visit the Royal 22e Régiment Museum.

d. Ursulines Monastery: Step into the Ursulines Monastery, North America's oldest institution of learning for women, and discover its captivating history and fascinating artifacts.

e. Quartier Petit Champlain: Stroll through the narrow streets of Quartier Petit Champlain, a picturesque neighborhood filled with boutiques, restaurants, and art galleries. Don't miss the famous Breakneck Stairs (Escalier Casse-Cou).

Historic Sites outside Old Quebec :
Beyond the confines of Old Quebec, there are several historic sites that provide further insights into Quebec City's past. Explore these noteworthy attractions to gain a comprehensive understanding of the region's heritage.

a. Plains of Abraham: Visit the Plains of Abraham, a historic battlefield where the famous Battle of Quebec took place in 1759. Enjoy the vast green spaces, statues, and the Plains of Abraham Museum.

b. Parliament Hill: Marvel at the imposing Parliament Building, an architectural masterpiece housing the provincial legislature. Take a guided tour to learn about Quebec's political history.

c. Montmorency Falls: Venture just outside the city to witness the awe-inspiring Montmorency Falls, which are taller than Niagara Falls. Take a cable car ride, cross the suspension bridge, or hike along the trails for stunning views.

d. Musée de la Civilisation: Immerse yourself in Quebec's rich cultural heritage at the Musée de la Civilisation. Explore its engaging exhibits, including the First Nations Gallery and the History of Quebec exhibit.

e. Maison Henry-Stuart: Step back in time at Maison Henry-Stuart, a meticulously restored 18th-century house. Gain insights into the daily lives of Quebec City's elite through the period rooms and exhibits.

Cultural Experiences and Festivals :

Quebec City is a vibrant hub of cultural experiences and festivals that celebrate its rich heritage throughout the year. Here are a few events that offer a unique glimpse into the city's traditions and customs.

a. Winter Carnival: Experience the magic of Quebec's Winter Carnival, one of the world's largest winter festivals. Enjoy ice sculptures, snow slides, parades, and traditional activities like ice canoe races.

b. New France Festival: Step into the 17th and 18th centuries during the New France Festival, where the streets of Old Quebec come alive with costumed characters, period shows, and reenactments.

c. Festival d'été de Québec: Join the celebration at the Festival d'été de Québec, a renowned music festival featuring international artists and diverse genres. Enjoy concerts at various outdoor venues across the city.

d. Quebec City Summer Festival: Delight in the lively atmosphere of the Quebec City Summer Festival, showcasing music, theater, street performances, and visual arts. Explore stages and exhibitions throughout the city.

French Cuisine and Shopping

Quebec City is a captivating destination that offers a unique blend of European charm and Canadian hospitality. Known as the cradle of French civilization in North America, Quebec City showcases a rich cultural heritage, breathtaking architecture, and a vibrant culinary scene. In this travel guide, we will delve into the world of French cuisine and explore the diverse shopping experiences that await visitors in this historic city.

I. French Cuisine in Quebec City:

Gastronomic Heritage:
a. Historical Influences: Quebec City's culinary traditions draw heavily from its French roots, with

recipes and techniques handed down through generations.

b. Signature Dishes: Poutine, tourtière (meat pie), cretons (pork spread), and maple syrup-infused delights like taffy and sugar pie are must-try dishes.

c. Iconic Restaurants: Le Continental, L'Initiale, and Aux Anciens Canadiens offer fine dining experiences that showcase French-inspired cuisine.

Local Food Markets:

a. Marché du Vieux-Port: Located near the Old Port, this bustling market showcases a wide array of fresh produce, local cheeses, meats, and artisanal products.

b. Marché du Vieux-Québec: Situated in the heart of Old Quebec, this indoor market offers a variety of regional specialties, including maple products and traditional French pastries.

Culinary Experiences:

a. Food Tours: Joining a guided food tour allows visitors to explore the city's culinary hotspots, taste local delicacies, and learn about the history and culture behind Quebec City's cuisine.

b. Cooking Classes: Several establishments offer cooking classes where participants can learn to prepare classic French dishes and gain insight into the secrets of authentic Quebecois cuisine.

II. Shopping in Quebec City:

Quartier Petit Champlain:
a. Cobblestone Streets and Boutiques: Known as one of the most picturesque neighborhoods in North America, Quartier Petit Champlain is lined with charming boutiques offering a wide range of goods, including clothing, jewelry, art, and souvenirs.
b. Local Artisans: Visitors can discover unique handcrafted items, such as pottery, leather goods, and artwork, created by talented local artisans.

Rue Saint-Jean:
a. Eclectic Shopping Experience: Rue Saint-Jean, stretching from Old Quebec to the vibrant Faubourg Saint-Jean neighborhood, is a vibrant street that caters to diverse shopping preferences.
b. Fashion and Specialty Stores: Visitors can explore trendy fashion boutiques, specialty shops offering gourmet food products, antique stores, and bookshops.

Laurier Québec:

a. Shopping Mall Experience: Laurier Québec is the largest shopping mall in Eastern Canada, featuring over 350 stores and a variety of dining options.
b. Fashion and Lifestyle Brands: Visitors can indulge in a wide range of fashion brands, from luxury labels to popular retail chains, as well as browse through electronics, home decor, and beauty products.

III. Exploring Quebec City:

Old Quebec:
a. UNESCO World Heritage Site: The historic district of Old Quebec exudes a captivating ambiance, with its cobblestone streets, 17th-century architecture, and fortified walls.
b. Landmarks and Attractions: Explore the iconic Château Frontenac, visit Place Royale, and wander through the charming streets of Petit Champlain, Rue du Trésor, and Rue Saint-Jean.

Montmorency Falls:
a. Natural Beauty: Just outside the city, Montmorency Falls showcases a majestic waterfall that stands taller than Niagara Falls.
b. Activities and Observation Points: Visitors can enjoy a cable car ride, hike along the surrounding

trails, or take in breathtaking views from the suspension bridge.

Festival Season:
a. Festivals and Events: Quebec City hosts a multitude of festivals throughout the year, including the Winter Carnival, Summer Festival, and New France Festival, offering visitors a chance to experience the city's vibrant cultural scene.

Quebec City, with its rich French heritage and captivating charm, offers a delightful fusion of French cuisine and diverse shopping experiences. From savoring traditional dishes to exploring local markets and strolling through quaint streets lined with unique boutiques, visitors can immerse themselves in the vibrant culture of this historic city. Whether it's indulging in a culinary adventure or discovering one-of-a-kind treasures, Quebec City promises a truly unforgettable travel experience.

CHAPTER FOUR

Natural Wonders of Canada

•*Niagara Falls*

Welcome to Canada, a country known for its natural beauty and breathtaking landscapes. One of the most iconic destinations in Canada is Niagara Falls, a true marvel of nature. Located on the border between Canada and the United States, Niagara Falls is a magnificent collection of waterfalls renowned for its awe-inspiring beauty and the thunderous roar of cascading water. In this comprehensive travel guide, we will take you on a journey through Niagara Falls, Canada, and uncover the many wonders and attractions this enchanting destination has to offer.

The Magnificence of Niagara Falls:

Niagara Falls comprises three majestic waterfalls: the Horseshoe Falls, American Falls, and Bridal Veil Falls. Towering water columns plunge dramatically into the Niagara River, creating an incredible spectacle that attracts millions of visitors each year. Marvel at the power of nature as you witness the sheer force and beauty of the falls, surrounded by mist and rainbows.

Exploring Niagara Falls State Park:
Start your adventure at Niagara Falls State Park, the oldest state park in the United States. As you traverse the park's well-maintained pathways, enjoy panoramic views of the falls from different vantage points. Don't miss the Cave of the Winds tour, which allows you to experience the falls up close and personal by descending into the Niagara Gorge and exploring the hurricane deck.

Journey Behind the Falls:
Embark on an unforgettable adventure by taking the Journey Behind the Falls tour. This unique experience provides visitors with the opportunity to venture into tunnels carved out of bedrock, leading to observation decks located directly behind the Horseshoe Falls. Prepare to be captivated by the thunderous roar and the extraordinary force of the falling water.

Maid of the Mist Boat Tour:
No visit to Niagara Falls would be complete without a Maid of the Mist boat tour. Put on your complimentary poncho and board the iconic boat

that will take you as close as possible to the thundering waters of the falls. Feel the mist on your face and hear the deafening roar as you witness the falls from an entirely new perspective.

Niagara Falls Illumination:
As the sun sets and darkness falls, Niagara Falls is transformed into a mesmerizing display of lights. The cascades are illuminated with vibrant colors, creating a captivating and magical atmosphere. Be sure to witness the illumination spectacle, which takes place every evening, and marvel at the sheer beauty of the falls under the night sky.

Niagara-on-the-Lake:
Just a short drive from Niagara Falls, you'll find the charming town of Niagara-on-the-Lake. Known for its picturesque streets lined with historic buildings and beautiful gardens, this quaint town offers a serene and romantic escape from the hustle and bustle. Explore the boutique shops, indulge in wine tasting at the local wineries, and catch a show at the renowned Shaw Festival Theatre.

Niagara Fallsview Casino Resort:
For those seeking entertainment and excitement, the Niagara Fallsview Casino Resort is a must-visit

destination. Try your luck at the gaming tables, enjoy world-class performances at the Avalon Theatre, or savor a delicious meal at one of the resort's many restaurants. The casino's prime location provides stunning views of the falls, making it a truly unique gaming experience.

Niagara SkyWheel:
For a bird's-eye view of Niagara Falls and its surroundings, take a ride on the Niagara SkyWheel. This towering Ferris wheel offers panoramic vistas of the falls, the city skyline, and the vast landscape beyond. Enjoy the breathtaking scenery while enclosed in climate-controlled gondolas, ensuring a comfortable experience no matter the weather.

Niagara Falls History Museum:
Delve into the rich history and heritage of the Niagara Falls region at the Niagara Falls History Museum. Explore fascinating exhibits that detail the geological formation of the falls, the daredevils who attempted daring stunts, and the cultural significance of this iconic natural wonder. Gain a deeper appreciation for the falls and the communities that have thrived alongside them.

Niagara Parks Botanical Gardens:

Escape the crowds and immerse yourself in nature's tranquility at the Niagara Parks Botanical Gardens. Located just a short distance from the falls, this 99-acre paradise is home to meticulously manicured gardens, stunning floral displays, and peaceful walking trails. Take a leisurely stroll, breathe in the fragrant air, and rejuvenate your senses amidst the natural beauty.

Visiting the Falls

Niagara Falls, one of Canada's most iconic landmarks, is a breathtaking natural wonder that attracts millions of visitors from around the world each year. Located on the border of Ontario, Canada, and New York, United States, this magnificent set of waterfalls offers an awe-inspiring spectacle of nature's power and beauty. In this travel guide, we will delve into the various aspects of visiting Niagara Falls, including its history, the best viewpoints, thrilling activities, nearby attractions, and practical tips to make the most of your trip.

A Glimpse into Niagara Falls' History:
Niagara Falls holds a rich historical significance that dates back centuries. The Indigenous peoples of the region, including the Ongiara and the Neutral Nation, revered the falls for their spiritual importance. European explorers, such as Samuel de Champlain and Father Louis Hennepin, encountered the falls in the 17th century, and their accounts helped popularize the destination. Over time, Niagara Falls evolved into a popular tourist attraction, prompting the establishment of parks, hotels, and recreational activities to cater to the growing number of visitors.

Exploring the Falls:
a. Horseshoe Falls: The most famous and awe-inspiring of the three waterfalls that comprise Niagara Falls is the Horseshoe Falls. This magnificent crescent-shaped cascade plunges over 167 feet (51 meters) and provides visitors with an immersive and thrilling experience.
b. American Falls: Located on the American side, this waterfall is equally impressive and can be admired from various viewpoints, including Prospect Point Park and Luna Island. Witness the raw power of the falls as millions of gallons of water thunder down its rocky face.

c. Bridal Veil Falls: The smallest of the three falls, Bridal Veil Falls is a delicate cascade located next to the American Falls. Although relatively less voluminous, it offers a mesmerizing sight as it gracefully descends into the Niagara River.

Best Viewpoints:

a. Journey Behind the Falls: Embark on an extraordinary adventure by venturing into tunnels that take you behind the cascading waters of the Horseshoe Falls. This unique vantage point provides an up-close encounter with the falls' immense power and beauty.

b. Hornblower Niagara Cruises: Hop aboard a Hornblower boat tour to witness the falls from an entirely different perspective. Sail along the Niagara River, getting closer to the thundering falls and feeling the misty spray on your face.

c. Skylon Tower Observation Deck: Soar to new heights by ascending the Skylon Tower, where a panoramic observation deck offers breathtaking vistas of the falls and the surrounding landscape. Capture stunning photographs and appreciate the vastness of this natural spectacle.

Thrilling Activities:

a. Whirlpool Aero Car: Experience the exhilaration of traversing the Niagara Gorge aboard the Whirlpool Aero Car. Suspended from sturdy cables, this antique cable car takes you across the turbulent waters, offering unparalleled views of the swirling rapids and the colossal whirlpool.

b. White Water Walk: Take a leisurely stroll along the White Water Walk boardwalk, situated along the Niagara River. Immerse yourself in the sheer power of the rapids as they crash against the rocks, creating a mesmerizing display of nature's force.

c. Niagara SkyWheel: For a more leisurely yet thrilling experience, take a ride on the Niagara SkyWheel. This giant Ferris wheel provides a bird's-eye view of the falls and the surrounding landscape, especially captivating during sunset or at night when the falls are illuminated.

Nearby Attractions:

a. Niagara-on-the-Lake: Just a short drive from Niagara Falls, this charming town offers a delightful escape. Known for its wineries, historic sites, and picturesque scenery, Niagara-on-the-Lake is a must-visit destination. Explore its quaint streets, indulge in wine tastings, or catch a play at the renowned Shaw Festival Theatre.

b. Niagara Falls State Park: On the American side, Niagara Falls State Park offers numerous trails, picnic areas, and viewpoints to enjoy the falls from a different perspective. Visit the Observation Tower for stunning views, or take a guided tour to learn about the area's geology and history.

c. Clifton Hill: If you're seeking a vibrant and lively atmosphere, head to Clifton Hill. This bustling entertainment district features a myriad of attractions, including museums, haunted houses, arcades, and themed restaurants. Enjoy the vibrant energy and embrace the carnival-like ambiance.

Practical Tips:

a. Timing and Crowds: Niagara Falls can be crowded during peak tourist seasons, such as summer. Consider visiting during the shoulder seasons (spring or fall) to avoid excessive crowds and long queues.

b. Border Crossing: If you plan to visit both the Canadian and American sides of the falls, ensure you have the necessary documentation for border crossing, such as a valid passport.

c. Weather Considerations: Be prepared for changing weather conditions, as mist and spray from the falls can create a damp environment.

Dress in layers and bring waterproof clothing to stay comfortable during your visit.

d. Accommodations and Dining: Niagara Falls offers a range of accommodations, from luxury hotels with falls views to budget-friendly options. Explore the diverse dining scene, with restaurants offering international cuisine, local delicacies, and stunning views of the falls.

Niagara-on-the-Lake

Nestled in the heart of Canada's wine country, Niagara-on-the-Lake is a picturesque town that exudes charm and beauty. Located just a short drive from the world-famous Niagara Falls, this quaint destination offers a delightful blend of history, culture, natural wonders, and culinary delights. In this Canada travel guide, we will take you on a journey through Niagara-on-the-Lake, showcasing its top attractions, activities, and hidden gems that make it a must-visit destination for any traveler.

History and Heritage:

Niagara-on-the-Lake boasts a rich history that dates back to the 18th century. Once the first capital of Upper Canada, the town is steeped in colonial heritage. Begin your exploration with a visit to Fort George National Historic Site, a meticulously restored fort that played a crucial role during the War of 1812. Take a guided tour and witness reenactments that bring history to life. Another notable historic site is the Niagara Historical Society & Museum, where you can delve deeper into the town's past through its fascinating exhibits.

Wineries and Wine Tasting:
Niagara-on-the-Lake is renowned for its vineyards and world-class wineries. Embark on a wine-tasting journey along the Niagara Wine Route, which encompasses over 20 wineries. Sample award-winning wines, learn about the winemaking process, and soak in the beautiful vineyard landscapes. Some notable wineries include Jackson-Triggs, Peller Estates, and Inniskillin. Don't forget to savor the region's signature ice wine, a sweet and luscious treat.

Shaw Festival:
Culture enthusiasts will delight in the Shaw Festival, a world-renowned theater event held annually from April to October. Dedicated to the works of George Bernard Shaw and his

contemporaries, the festival showcases a repertoire of plays performed by a talented ensemble of actors. From classic dramas to light-hearted comedies, the Shaw Festival offers a diverse selection of performances that captivate audiences from around the globe.

Niagara Parkway:

Take a scenic drive along the Niagara Parkway, a picturesque road that follows the Niagara River. Marvel at stunning vistas, well-manicured gardens, and historic landmarks along the way. Stop by Queenston Heights Park, where you can hike to the top of Brock's Monument, commemorating Major-General Sir Isaac Brock, a hero of the War of 1812. As you continue along the parkway, be sure to visit the Floral Clock, a floral masterpiece that displays intricate designs created using thousands of colorful blooms.

Niagara-on-the-Lake Heritage District:

The town's heritage district is a charming area filled with beautifully preserved 19th-century buildings housing unique shops, boutiques, and art galleries. Stroll along Queen Street, the main thoroughfare, and explore the local craftsmanship, jewelry, antiques, and gourmet food stores. Indulge in delectable treats at the Olde Angel Inn, a historic pub dating back to 1789, or enjoy a traditional English tea experience at one of the cozy tearooms.

Outdoor Activities:

Nature enthusiasts will find plenty of outdoor activities to enjoy in Niagara-on-the-Lake. Take a leisurely bike ride along the Niagara River Recreation Trail, which offers breathtaking views of the river and passes through vineyards and orchards. You can also go on a relaxing boat tour or kayak excursion along the Niagara River or join a scenic helicopter ride for a bird's-eye view of the region's beauty. During the summer months, catch a performance at the Niagara-on-the-Lake Court House, where the annual Music Niagara festival showcases exceptional musical talent.

Culinary Delights:

Niagara-on-the-Lake is a paradise for food lovers, offering a range of dining experiences that cater to all tastes. From elegant fine dining restaurants to charming bistros and cozy cafes, the town's culinary scene is diverse and vibrant. Indulge in farm-to-table cuisine using locally sourced ingredients, savor artisanal cheeses, and enjoy the freshest seafood. Don't forget to pair your meals with the region's exquisite wines for a truly unforgettable gastronomic experience.

Adventure Activities

Niagara Falls, one of the most awe-inspiring natural wonders of the world, attracts millions of visitors each year with its breathtaking beauty and magnificent cascades. Situated on the border of Canada and the United States, the falls offer an array of adventure activities that provide an adrenaline rush like no other. In this Canada travel guide, we will delve into the thrilling adventure opportunities available at Niagara Falls, exploring everything from high-speed boat tours and helicopter rides to ziplining and hiking adventures. Embark on an unforgettable journey filled with excitement, natural beauty, and heart-pounding experiences at Niagara Falls.

Maid of the Mist Boat Tour:
The iconic Maid of the Mist boat tour is a must-do activity for any visitor to Niagara Falls. Don a blue

poncho and embark on a thrilling voyage to the base of the falls, where you'll witness the sheer power and beauty of the cascading water. Feel the mist on your face as you get up close and personal with the thunderous roar of the falls. The Maid of the Mist boat tour promises an immersive and awe-inspiring experience that will leave you breathless.

Journey Behind the Falls:

For a unique perspective on Niagara Falls, consider taking the Journey Behind the Falls tour. Descend deep into the bedrock and venture through a series of tunnels that lead to observation decks located directly behind the roaring curtain of water. Feel the ground tremble beneath your feet as you witness the raw power of the falls from a whole new angle. The Journey Behind the Falls tour provides an up-close encounter with the natural forces at play, leaving visitors in awe of the sheer magnitude of Niagara Falls.

Helicopter Rides:

For those seeking a bird's-eye view of the falls, helicopter rides offer an exhilarating adventure. Soar high above the roaring waters as you capture breathtaking panoramic views of the falls, the

Niagara River, and the surrounding landscapes. The thrilling sensation of hovering above the cascades provides an unmatched perspective and an unforgettable experience. Helicopter rides at Niagara Falls are a popular choice for those who wish to combine adventure, stunning visuals, and a touch of luxury.

Whirlpool Jet Boat Tours:
If you crave an adrenaline-pumping adventure, a Whirlpool Jet Boat tour is the perfect choice. Climb aboard a powerful jet boat and prepare for a wild and wet ride through the Niagara Gorge. Experience heart-stopping 360-degree spins, surges of speed, and thrilling rapids as you navigate the treacherous waters of the Niagara River. The combination of adrenaline-inducing maneuvers and the stunning natural surroundings make the Whirlpool Jet Boat tour an unforgettable adventure.

Ziplining and Aerial Adventures :
For those seeking a unique way to appreciate the beauty of Niagara Falls, ziplining and aerial adventures offer an exhilarating experience. Soar through the sky on a zipline, enjoying breathtaking views of the falls and the surrounding landscape.

Some zipline experiences even allow participants to dangle over the mighty Niagara River, adding an extra thrill to the adventure. Additionally, aerial adventure parks offer a range of activities such as suspended bridges, tightropes, and obstacle courses that allow visitors to navigate the treetops and immerse themselves in nature.

•Rocky Mountains

Nestled in the heart of North America, the Canadian Rockies stand as an awe-inspiring testament to the wonders of nature. Stretching across the western provinces of British Columbia and Alberta, this magnificent mountain range offers a plethora of experiences for adventure enthusiasts, nature lovers, and curious travelers alike. From towering peaks to turquoise lakes, from majestic glaciers to charming alpine towns, the Canadian Rockies beckon visitors to embark on a journey of discovery and enchantment. In this travel guide, we will delve into the beauty, attractions, activities, and practical information to help you make the most of your visit to the Rocky Mountains in Canada.

Geography and Natural Wonders:

The Canadian Rockies form a part of the larger North American Rocky Mountain range, extending approximately 1,500 kilometers (930 miles) from the northernmost region of British Columbia to the southern boundary of Alberta. This majestic mountain range is characterized by its rugged terrain, towering peaks, and pristine alpine environments. Within the Canadian Rockies, you will encounter an array of natural wonders, including Banff National Park, Jasper National Park, Yoho National Park, Kootenay National Park, and Waterton Lakes National Park. These protected areas are home to breathtaking glaciers, thundering waterfalls, emerald lakes, and diverse wildlife, offering endless opportunities for exploration and outdoor adventures.

Banff National Park:

Located in Alberta, Banff National Park is Canada's oldest national park and a UNESCO World Heritage Site. With its awe-inspiring landscapes and abundant wildlife, Banff attracts millions of visitors each year. The town of Banff serves as a gateway to the park and offers a charming mix of accommodations, restaurants, and shops. Must-visit attractions in Banff National Park include Lake Louise, Moraine Lake, Johnston Canyon, and the iconic Banff Springs Hotel. Outdoor enthusiasts can indulge in activities such as hiking, wildlife spotting, camping, canoeing, and skiing in the winter months.

Jasper National Park:
Adjacent to Banff National Park, Jasper National Park is another jewel in the Canadian Rockies' crown. Renowned for its untouched wilderness and stunning vistas, Jasper offers a more tranquil and less crowded experience compared to its neighboring park. The Icefields Parkway, a scenic highway connecting Banff and Jasper, is an absolute must-drive route, offering jaw-dropping views of glaciers, turquoise lakes, and rugged peaks. Popular attractions in Jasper National Park include Maligne Lake, Athabasca Falls, Mount Edith Cavell, and the Columbia Icefield, where you can walk on the Athabasca Glacier.

Yoho and Kootenay National Parks:
Yoho National Park, situated in British Columbia, captivates visitors with its dramatic landscapes and diverse ecosystems. The park is known for its impressive waterfalls, including the iconic Takakkaw Falls, and the stunning Emerald Lake,

which boasts vivid turquoise waters surrounded by towering peaks. Kootenay National Park, also in British Columbia, offers a quieter and more off-the-beaten-path experience. Its highlights include the Marble Canyon, Vermilion River, and the Radium Hot Springs.

Waterton Lakes National Park:

Nestled in the southwestern corner of Alberta, Waterton Lakes National Park is a hidden gem renowned for its breathtaking mountain scenery and tranquil lakes. This park shares the Canada-United States border with Glacier National Park, forming the Waterton-Glacier International Peace Park, a UNESCO World Heritage Site. Visitors can explore stunning trails, cruise on the sparkling waters of Upper Waterton Lake, and spot diverse wildlife, including bears, elk, and bighorn sheep.

Outdoor Activities and Adventure:

The Canadian Rockies provide an abundance of opportunities for outdoor enthusiasts. Hiking trails crisscross the mountains, ranging from gentle walks suitable for all fitness levels to challenging multi-day treks. Canoeing, kayaking, and rafting are popular activities on the lakes and rivers, while wildlife safaris and guided tours offer unique insights into the region's flora and fauna. In winter, skiing, snowboarding, and snowshoeing are favorite pastimes in world-class resorts like Banff, Lake Louise, and Jasper.

Cultural Experiences and Local Communities:

Beyond its natural splendor, the Canadian Rockies are also home to vibrant communities and a rich cultural heritage. The towns of Banff and Jasper offer a range of cultural attractions, including museums, art galleries, and heritage sites. Visitors can immerse themselves in the local culture by attending festivals, exploring indigenous heritage centers, or experiencing traditional cuisine. The Rocky Mountains serve as a backdrop for numerous cultural events throughout the year, providing a unique blend of natural and cultural experiences.

Practical Information:

a. Transportation: The Canadian Rockies are well-connected by roadways, with highways providing access to the major national parks. Calgary International Airport and Edmonton International Airport serve as gateways to the region.

b. Accommodations: From luxury resorts to cozy mountain lodges and campgrounds, a wide range of accommodations are available to suit every budget and preference.

c. Weather and Seasons: The Rockies experience distinct seasons, with warm summers, colorful autumns, snowy winters, and mild springs. It is advisable to check weather conditions and pack accordingly.

d. Wildlife and Safety: The Canadian Rockies are home to diverse wildlife, including bears, elk, and mountain goats. Visitors should follow safety guidelines and respect wildlife habitats.

e. Permits and Fees: National parks in Canada require entry fees, and some activities may require permits. It is essential to check park websites for up-to-date information.

Banff National Park

Nestled in the heart of the Canadian Rockies, Banff National Park stands as a testament to the unparalleled beauty and awe-inspiring landscapes of the Great White North. Spanning over 6,600 square kilometers, Banff is Canada's oldest national park and a UNESCO World Heritage Site. With its breathtaking mountain ranges, pristine turquoise lakes, and diverse wildlife, this natural wonderland attracts millions of visitors from around the globe every year. In this comprehensive travel guide, we will delve into the wonders of Banff National Park, exploring its geological marvels, outdoor adventures, and cultural highlights.

History and Location:
Banff National Park was established in 1885, making it Canada's first national park and the third oldest in the world. Situated in the province of Alberta, Banff is located approximately 128 kilometers west of Calgary, making it easily accessible for both domestic and international travelers. The park is part of the larger Canadian Rocky Mountain Parks, which also includes Jasper, Kootenay, and Yoho national parks, forming a continuous protected area along the majestic Rocky Mountains.

Natural Beauty and Geological Marvels:
Banff National Park boasts a remarkable array of natural wonders that leave visitors in awe of the

Earth's majestic creations. Towering snow-capped peaks, including the iconic Mount Rundle and Cascade Mountain, provide a breathtaking backdrop to the stunning landscapes. The park is also home to the Columbia Icefield, one of the largest icefields in North America, feeding glaciers that carve their way through the mountains.

The jewel of Banff National Park is undoubtedly Lake Louise, renowned for its ethereal turquoise waters reflecting the surrounding mountain peaks. Moraine Lake, with its vibrant blue hue and the Valley of the Ten Peaks as a backdrop, is equally mesmerizing. These iconic lakes offer breathtaking vistas and numerous opportunities for hiking, kayaking, and photography.

Wildlife and Biodiversity:
Banff National Park is a sanctuary for a rich variety of wildlife species, offering visitors the chance to encounter them in their natural habitats. The park is home to grizzly bears, black bears, elk, moose, wolves, and cougars, among many other species. The best chances of spotting these magnificent creatures are during the early morning or evening hours, particularly along the Bow Valley Parkway and Icefields Parkway. Wildlife tours and guided

hikes are available for those seeking a closer look at the park's inhabitants while ensuring their safety.

Outdoor Adventures:

Banff National Park is a paradise for outdoor enthusiasts, offering a plethora of activities that cater to all ages and skill levels. Hiking is a popular pursuit, with a vast network of trails crisscrossing the park, ranging from easy walks to challenging multi-day treks. The Plain of Six Glaciers Trail and the Sulphur Mountain Trail are among the most rewarding hikes, offering breathtaking views of glaciers, alpine meadows, and cascading waterfalls.

For those seeking an adrenaline rush, Banff National Park offers thrilling opportunities for rock climbing, mountain biking, and whitewater rafting. Lake Louise and nearby Lake Minnewanka are perfect for canoeing and kayaking, allowing visitors to immerse themselves in the tranquility of the park's pristine waters.

Cultural Highlights:

Banff National Park is not only a haven for nature enthusiasts but also a place of cultural significance. The town of Banff, situated within the park, offers a blend of history, art, and culture. The Banff Park

Museum, established in 1895, showcases an extensive collection of preserved animals and plants, providing insight into the park's natural heritage. The Whyte Museum of the Canadian Rockies celebrates the region's art, history, and culture through exhibitions and educational programs.

Additionally, the Banff Centre for Arts and Creativity hosts various cultural events, including concerts, exhibitions, and workshops, making it a hub for artistic expression and creativity. Visitors can immerse themselves in the vibrant cultural scene while enjoying the splendor of the surrounding natural landscapes.

Jasper National Park

Nestled in the heart of the Canadian Rockies, Jasper National Park is a true natural wonderland. With its majestic mountains, pristine turquoise lakes, abundant wildlife, and breathtaking glaciers, it is a haven for outdoor enthusiasts and nature lovers. In this Canada travel guide, we invite you to explore the beauty and adventure that await you in Jasper National Park.

Geographical Overview:

Jasper National Park is located in the province of Alberta, Canada, spanning an area of 11,000 square kilometers. It is the largest national park in the Canadian Rockies and forms part of the UNESCO World Heritage site, Canadian Rocky Mountain Parks. The park boasts a diverse range of landscapes, including rugged peaks, deep valleys, cascading waterfalls, and dense forests.

Natural Attractions

Jasper National Park offers an array of natural attractions that will leave you spellbound. One of the park's iconic landmarks is the Columbia Icefield, which is home to several stunning glaciers, including the Athabasca Glacier. Visitors can take guided tours or embark on glacier walks to witness the awe-inspiring ice formations up close.

The park is also renowned for its crystal-clear lakes, such as Maligne Lake and Pyramid Lake, which offer unparalleled beauty. Rent a canoe or kayak and glide across the serene waters, surrounded by towering mountains and dense forests. Wildlife enthusiasts will be thrilled by the chance to spot grizzly bears, black bears, elk, moose, and mountain goats roaming freely in their natural habitat.

Outdoor Activities :

Jasper National Park is a playground for outdoor enthusiasts, providing a plethora of activities for all ages and skill levels. Hiking is a favorite pastime here, with numerous trails catering to different abilities. The Skyline Trail offers a multi-day trek through alpine meadows and stunning vistas, while the Valley of the Five Lakes provides a shorter, family-friendly option.

For those seeking a more adrenaline-fueled adventure, whitewater rafting on the Athabasca River promises an exhilarating experience. The park's extensive network of biking trails also offers opportunities for cycling enthusiasts to explore the wilderness at their own pace.

During the winter months, Jasper National Park transforms into a winter wonderland. Cross-country skiing, snowshoeing, and ice climbing are just a few of the activities that winter sports enthusiasts can enjoy. The Marmot Basin ski area, located within the park, offers world-class downhill skiing and snowboarding, catering to all levels of expertise.

Indigenous Culture and History:
Jasper National Park is not only a haven for natural beauty but also a place of rich Indigenous history. The park is situated within the traditional territories of several Indigenous groups, including the Nakoda, Cree, and Métis peoples. Visitors have the opportunity to learn about and appreciate the cultural heritage of these communities through interpretive programs, guided walks, and Indigenous art displays.

Accommodation and Amenities:
Jasper National Park offers a range of accommodation options to suit every traveler's needs. From cozy lodges and rustic cabins to campgrounds and RV parks, there are options for all budgets and preferences. The town of Jasper, located within the park, provides a variety of amenities, including restaurants, shops, and visitor centers where you can gather information and plan your adventures.

Conservation and Sustainability :

Jasper National Park is committed to preserving its pristine environment and promoting sustainable tourism practices. The park has implemented initiatives to minimize the ecological footprint of visitors, such as waste management programs and the promotion of eco-friendly transportation options. Travelers are encouraged to follow Leave No Trace principles and respect wildlife and their natural habitats.

Wildlife Viewing and Hiking

Canada's Rocky Mountains offer an awe-inspiring natural playground, teeming with diverse wildlife and offering unparalleled opportunities for hiking enthusiasts. Spanning across the provinces of Alberta and British Columbia, this iconic mountain range attracts nature lovers and adventurers from around the world. In this comprehensive travel guide, we will delve into the wonders of wildlife viewing and hiking experiences in the Canadian Rocky Mountains, providing you with essential information to make the most of your journey.

Discovering the Canadian Rocky Mountains:

Geography and highlights of the Canadian Rocky Mountains.

Popular national parks and protected areas: Banff National Park, Jasper National Park, Yoho National Park, and Kootenay National Park. Importance of conservation efforts in preserving the region's unique ecosystem.

Wildlife Viewing in the Canadian Rockies:

Overview of wildlife species: grizzly bears, black bears, moose, elk, mountain goats, bighorn sheep, wolves, and more.

Best wildlife viewing seasons and locations within the Rocky Mountains.

Guided tours, safaris, and self-guided opportunities for observing wildlife.

Responsible wildlife viewing practices and guidelines.

Hiking Adventures in the Canadian Rocky Mountains:

Trail options for all skill levels, from leisurely walks to challenging multi-day treks.

Must-visit hiking trails: Lake Louise, Moraine Lake, Plain of Six Glaciers, Wilcox Pass, Berg Lake Trail, and West Coast Trail.

Essential hiking gear and safety precautions to consider.

Permits and regulations for overnight camping and backcountry hiking.

Planning Your Trip to the Canadian Rockies:

Best time to visit based on weather, wildlife activity, and crowd levels.

Transportation options: airports, car rentals, and public transportation.

Accommodation choices: hotels, lodges, campgrounds, and backcountry camping.

Local resources, visitor centers, and guided tour operators.

Captivating Side Activities:

Scenic drives along the Icefields Parkway and the Trans-Canada Highway.

Exploring stunning waterfalls, such as Takakkaw Falls and Athabasca Falls.

Engaging in water sports like canoeing, kayaking, and fishing in the pristine mountain lakes and rivers.

Winter activities, including skiing, snowboarding, and ice climbing.
Indigenous Culture and History:

Recognizing the rich heritage of the Indigenous peoples in the Canadian Rockies.
Indigenous-led tours and cultural experiences.
Preservation of ancient rock art and historical sites.
Sustainability and Responsible Tourism:

Promoting sustainable practices to minimize environmental impact.
Supporting local communities and Indigenous businesses.
Leave No Trace principles and responsible waste management.

Safety Tips and Considerations:

Weather conditions and mountain hazards.
Wildlife encounters and safety precautions.
Navigation and trail etiquette.
Emergency services and communication in remote areas.

•Pacific Coastline

Tofino and Ucluelet

Nestled on the western shores of Vancouver Island in British Columbia, Canada, the picturesque towns of Tofino and Ucluelet beckon travelers with their awe-inspiring natural beauty. These neighboring communities are blessed with pristine beaches, ancient rainforests, and a diverse array of wildlife, making them a paradise for outdoor enthusiasts and nature lovers. In this comprehensive travel guide, we will delve into the wonders of Tofino and Ucluelet, exploring their attractions, outdoor activities, culinary delights, and accommodations, providing you with all the information you need to embark on an unforgettable adventure.

I. Discovering Tofino:
A. Location and Accessibility:
Situated at the western edge of Vancouver Island, Tofino is approximately 194 kilometers (120 miles) from Nanaimo and 316 kilometers (196 miles) from Victoria. Travelers can reach Tofino by ferry and road, or by air through the Tofino-Long Beach Airport.

B. Beaches and Coastal Landscapes:
Tofino boasts stunning beaches that stretch along the coastline, offering breathtaking vistas and opportunities for leisurely strolls, beachcombing, and sunbathing. Long Beach, Chesterman Beach, and Cox Bay Beach are among the most popular beaches, each with its own unique charm.

C. Pacific Rim National Park Reserve:
Adjacent to Tofino, the Pacific Rim National Park Reserve is a haven for nature enthusiasts. This pristine park encompasses temperate rainforests, rugged coastal trails, and serene lakes. Visitors can explore the rainforest trails, marvel at the ancient trees, and embark on unforgettable kayaking adventures.

D. Wildlife Encounters:
Tofino is renowned for its abundant wildlife. Take a boat tour to witness the majestic gray whales on their annual migration, or spot black bears foraging along the shoreline. Birdwatchers will also be delighted by the diverse avian species that call this area home.

E. Surfing Capital of Canada:

With its powerful waves and pristine breaks, Tofino has earned its reputation as the surfing capital of Canada. Whether you are a seasoned surfer or a beginner, you can take advantage of the surf schools and rental shops that cater to all skill levels.

F. Culinary Delights:
Indulge your taste buds in Tofino's thriving culinary scene. From ocean-to-table seafood restaurants to cozy cafes and breweries, you can savor fresh, locally sourced ingredients while enjoying stunning ocean views.

G. Accommodations:
Tofino offers a range of accommodations, from luxury resorts to cozy cabins and bed and breakfasts. Whether you seek beachfront accommodations or a retreat nestled in the rainforest, there are options to suit every traveler's preferences and budget.

II. Exploring Ucluelet:
A. Location and Accessibility:
Located approximately 40 kilometers (25 miles) southeast of Tofino, Ucluelet can be accessed via the scenic Pacific Rim Highway. Travelers can also

fly into the Tofino-Long Beach Airport and take a short drive to Ucluelet.

B. Wild Pacific Trail:
Ucluelet is best known for its captivating Wild Pacific Trail, a 10-kilometer (6.2-mile) network of coastal paths that wind through ancient rainforests and rugged cliffs. The trail offers breathtaking views of the Pacific Ocean and its dramatic shoreline, providing ample opportunities for hiking, photography, and wildlife spotting.

C. Lighthouse Loop:
Within the Wild Pacific Trail, the Lighthouse Loop showcases the Amphitrite Point Lighthouse, a picturesque beacon that overlooks the crashing waves. This enchanting walk combines natural beauty with historical significance.

D. Barkley Sound:
Ucluelet serves as a gateway to Barkley Sound, a scenic marine area renowned for its fishing, kayaking, and boating opportunities. Explore the tranquil waters, visit the Broken Group Islands, or try your hand at catching salmon or halibut.

E. Terrace Beach and Little Beach:

Ucluelet is home to two beautiful beaches: Terrace Beach and Little Beach. These hidden gems offer tranquility and seclusion, with tide pools teeming with marine life and stunning vistas that will leave you in awe.

F. Arts and Culture:
Ucluelet celebrates its rich cultural heritage through various art galleries and museums. Immerse yourself in local Indigenous art and learn about the history and traditions of the region's First Nations communities.

G. Accommodations:
Ucluelet offers a range of accommodations, including seaside resorts, cozy inns, and vacation rentals. Whether you seek a luxurious getaway or a family-friendly retreat, Ucluelet provides options that cater to every traveler's needs.

III. Day Trips and Additional Activities:
A. Hot Springs Cove:
Embark on a memorable day trip from Tofino or Ucluelet to Hot Springs Cove, a natural hot spring located within the Maquinna Provincial Park. Accessible by boat or seaplane, this geothermal

treasure offers a unique opportunity to relax and rejuvenate amidst coastal rainforest scenery.

B. Meares Island:
Visit Meares Island, an unspoiled wilderness that is home to the majestic cedar trees, including the legendary "Big Tree." Take a guided hike or kayak excursion to immerse yourself in the ancient splendor of the island.

C. Whale Watching:
Both Tofino and Ucluelet offer exceptional whale-watching experiences. Hop aboard a boat tour to witness the awe-inspiring behavior of orcas, humpback whales, and other marine mammals in their natural habitat.

Tofino and Ucluelet captivate visitors with their stunning coastal landscapes, pristine beaches, and abundant wildlife. Whether you seek adventure, relaxation, or a blend of both, these charming communities offer a wealth of opportunities for exploration. From surfing to hiking, wildlife encounters to hot springs, Tofino and Ucluelet provide a diverse range of activities and experiences. Immerse yourself in the natural wonders, savor the local cuisine, and embrace the laid-back coastal lifestyle. Prepare for an unforgettable journey through the coastal beauty of Tofino and Ucluelet, where nature's wonders await at every turn.

Whale Watching

Canada's Pacific coastlines offer an enchanting opportunity for travelers to witness the majestic beauty of whales in their natural habitat. With its diverse marine ecosystem and abundant whale populations, this region has become a top destination for whale watching enthusiasts from around the world. This travel guide will provide comprehensive information on whale watching experiences along the Pacific coastlines of Canada, including the best locations, whale species, the ideal time to visit, ethical considerations, and other relevant details.

The Pacific Coastlines of Canada

Spanning over 27,000 kilometers, Canada's Pacific coastlines extend from British Columbia's

Vancouver Island to the northern reaches of Alaska. This vast stretch of coastline encompasses numerous stunning destinations that are renowned for their whale watching opportunities, including Victoria, Tofino, Telegraph Cove, and Prince Rupert.

Whale Species
The Pacific waters off Canada's coastlines are home to a rich variety of whale species. The most commonly spotted whales include the magnificent orcas (also known as killer whales), humpback whales, gray whales, minke whales, and the elusive fin whales. Each species offers a unique and awe-inspiring sight, making whale watching experiences in this region truly unforgettable.

Best Locations for Whale Watching
a. Victoria: Located on Vancouver Island, Victoria is one of the premier whale watching destinations in Canada. The calm waters of the Salish Sea offer excellent opportunities to observe orcas and other marine wildlife up close.

b. Tofino: Nestled within the stunning Clayoquot Sound, Tofino offers a combination of breathtaking landscapes and remarkable whale watching opportunities. Gray whales, humpback whales, and orcas frequently pass through these waters during their migratory journeys.

c. Telegraph Cove: Situated on Northern Vancouver Island, Telegraph Cove is a picturesque village that serves as a gateway to the wilderness of the Broughton Archipelago. This area is renowned for its orca sightings, as well as encounters with other marine wildlife such as dolphins and porpoises.

d. Prince Rupert: Located in British Columbia's northern region, Prince Rupert provides a unique whale watching experience. Here, travelers can witness the annual migration of humpback whales, as well as spot orcas and other marine species amidst the scenic coastal fjords.

Ideal Time to Visit
The best time for whale watching on Canada's Pacific coastlines varies depending on the species and their migratory patterns. Generally, the peak season runs from May to October, with different periods offering unique opportunities:
May to June: During this time, gray whales pass through the region on their northbound migration,

and orcas are frequently spotted. Humpback whales also begin to arrive.

July to September: These months offer optimal chances to witness humpback whales, as they spend the summer feeding in the nutrient-rich waters. Orca sightings continue, and other whale species, such as minke whales, may also be observed.

October: As the season nears its end, the waters become an active feeding ground for humpback whales, attracting them in significant numbers.

Ethical Considerations

Responsible whale watching is essential to preserve the well-being of these magnificent creatures and their habitats. When engaging in whale watching activities, it is important to choose tour operators who follow guidelines that prioritize the welfare of the animals. These guidelines include maintaining a safe distance from the whales, reducing boat speed in their presence, and avoiding any behavior that may disrupt their natural behavior.

Additional Tips and Recommendations

Dress in layers and bring appropriate clothing to stay warm and comfortable during your whale watching adventure.

Consider using binoculars or a camera with a telephoto lens to get a closer view of the whales without disturbing them.

Research and book your whale watching tour in advance to secure your spot and ensure a seamless experience.

Be prepared for the unpredictable nature of wildlife encounters. While sightings are common, they cannot be guaranteed.

Respect the marine environment by refraining from littering and following sustainable practices.

Whale watching on Canada's Pacific coastlines offers an awe-inspiring and unforgettable experience for travelers. With its diverse marine ecosystems, abundant whale populations, and numerous prime locations, this region has become a sought-after destination for nature enthusiasts. By following ethical guidelines and choosing reputable tour operators, visitors can witness these magnificent creatures in their natural habitat while ensuring their conservation for generations to come. Plan your trip to Canada's Pacific coastlines and embark on a whale watching adventure that will leave you with lifelong memories of these gentle giants of the sea.

Scenic drives and beaches

Canada's Pacific coastline offers an abundance of natural beauty, with stunning scenic drives and pristine beaches that are sure to captivate any traveler. From the rugged mountains of British Columbia to the charming coastal towns of Vancouver Island, this region is a paradise for those seeking breathtaking landscapes and tranquil seaside retreats. In this travel guide, we will delve into the most scenic drives and exquisite beaches along Canada's Pacific coast, presenting you with a comprehensive itinerary to make the most of your coastal adventure.

I. Scenic Drives:
A. Sea-to-Sky Highway:

Route overview and highlights.
Whistler: An alpine wonderland.
Shannon Falls Provincial Park: Majestic waterfalls.

Britannia Mine Museum: Immersive mining history.
B. Pacific Rim Highway:
Exploring Vancouver Island's rugged west coast.
Tofino: A charming surf town.
Pacific Rim National Park Reserve: Ancient rainforests and sandy beaches.
Long Beach: Surfing and stunning sunsets.
C. Sunshine Coast:
Serene coastal drive from Vancouver to Lund.
Gibsons: Quaint waterfront village.
Sechelt: Artistic community and scenic vistas.
Powell River: Outdoor adventures and historic sites.

II. Beaches:

A. Chesterman Beach, Tofino:

Vast sandy shores and picturesque surroundings.
Surfing, beachcombing, and storm-watching.
Wildlife encounters and tidal pool exploration.
B. Rathtrevor Beach, Parksville:
Sandy beach with warm shallow waters.
Ideal for swimming, sunbathing, and picnicking.
Nearby Rathtrevor Beach Provincial Park and trails.
C. Cox Bay Beach, Tofino:
World-class surf break and pristine beauty.

Beach activities, including paddleboarding and beachcombing.
Surrounded by stunning coastal scenery and wildlife.
D. Chesterman Beach, Tofino:
Vast sandy shores and picturesque surroundings.
Surfing, beachcombing, and storm-watching.
Wildlife encounters and tidal pool exploration.
E. Wickaninnish Beach, Tofino:
Iconic beach with dramatic coastal views.
Tranquil and secluded atmosphere.
Tide pool exploration and beach walks.

Canada's Pacific coastline is a treasure trove of scenic drives and breathtaking beaches, offering an unparalleled opportunity to immerse oneself in nature's wonders. From the captivating Sea-to-Sky Highway to the enchanting Pacific Rim Highway and the tranquil Sunshine Coast, each route presents unique landscapes, cultural experiences, and outdoor adventures. The region's pristine beaches, such as Chesterman Beach, Rathtrevor Beach, Cox Bay Beach, and Wickaninnish Beach, are ideal for relaxation, water sports, and wildlife encounters. Whether you're seeking the thrill of exploring rugged coastal terrain or simply yearning for a serene seaside getaway, the Pacific coast of

Canada promises to leave you awe-inspired and rejuvenated. Embark on this remarkable journey, and let the Pacific waves and breathtaking vistas create memories that will last a lifetime.

CHAPTER FIVE

Cultural Experiences

•*Indigenous Culture*

Canada is a land blessed with diverse landscapes, stunning natural beauty, and a rich cultural tapestry. At the heart of this vibrant nation lies the indigenous peoples, who have inhabited these lands for thousands of years. With over 600 distinct indigenous communities, each with its own unique traditions, languages, and art forms, Canada offers an extraordinary opportunity for travelers to immerse themselves in the fascinating world of Indigenous culture. In this travel guide, we will delve into the depths of Canada's Indigenous heritage, exploring its history, art, spirituality, and the meaningful experiences that await those who wish to discover and honor this ancient culture.

Historical Context:

To truly understand Canada's Indigenous culture, it is crucial to appreciate its historical context. The Indigenous peoples, including First Nations, Inuit, and Métis, have a profound connection to the land, tracing their roots back thousands of years. This section will provide an overview of their history, touching upon topics such as pre-colonial times, European contact, the impact of colonization, and the journey towards reconciliation.

Cultural Diversity:

Canada's Indigenous culture is remarkably diverse, with each community boasting its own unique traditions and customs. From the Haida of the Pacific Northwest to the Mi'kmaq of the Atlantic coast, this section will showcase some of the major Indigenous groups across Canada, highlighting their distinctive languages, art forms, traditional clothing, and culinary practices. Travelers will gain insights into the intricacies of Indigenous culture and appreciate the depth of knowledge and spirituality that has been passed down through generations.

Indigenous Art and Crafts:

Indigenous art is an integral part of the cultural fabric of Canada. This section will explore the various art forms practiced by Indigenous communities, including carving, beadwork, basket weaving, pottery, and painting. It will delve into the symbolism and storytelling embedded within these artistic expressions, as well as provide information on renowned Indigenous artists and artisans. Travelers will also find recommendations on where to visit galleries, cultural centers, and art festivals to witness the beauty and craftsmanship firsthand.

Traditional Indigenous Cuisine:
Indigenous cuisine reflects the deep connection between people and the land. In this section, travelers will have the opportunity to explore the traditional food practices of different Indigenous communities, such as the use of local ingredients, traditional cooking methods, and the significance of communal meals. Additionally, the guide will feature recommendations on Indigenous-owned restaurants and eateries across Canada, where visitors can savor a range of flavors and experience the unique culinary heritage of the First Peoples.

Indigenous Festivals and Events:

Throughout the year, Canada comes alive with vibrant Indigenous festivals and events that celebrate the culture, art, and traditions of the First Peoples. This section will highlight some of the most significant festivals, such as the Calgary Stampede's First Nations events, the National Indigenous Peoples Day celebrations, and the Inuvik Drum Dance Festival. Travelers will be provided with insights into the significance of these events and recommendations on where to experience them firsthand.

Indigenous Spiritual Practices:

Spirituality plays a profound role in Indigenous culture, encompassing a deep reverence for the natural world and a strong connection to ancestral wisdom. This section will delve into the spiritual beliefs and practices of Indigenous communities, such as smudging ceremonies, sweat lodges, and powwows. It will guide travelers in understanding the cultural protocols and etiquette when participating in these sacred ceremonies, emphasizing the importance of respect, understanding, and openness.

Indigenous Tourism Experiences:

For those seeking immersive cultural experiences, this section will offer a range of Indigenous tourism opportunities across Canada. From guided tours of historical sites and sacred lands to cultural workshops, visitors will have the chance to engage directly with Indigenous communities, learn traditional skills, hear captivating stories, and forge meaningful connections with the First Peoples. The guide will include information on Indigenous-led tour operators, cultural centers, and heritage sites, empowering travelers to make respectful and responsible choices during their journey.

Embarking on a journey to explore Canada's Indigenous culture is a gateway to a profound understanding of the land's history, spirituality, and diverse traditions. Through this travel guide, visitors will gain insights into the rich heritage of the First Peoples and discover ways to engage with Indigenous communities in a respectful and meaningful manner. By embracing the teachings of the past, we can contribute to the ongoing process of reconciliation and celebrate the vibrant tapestry of Canada's Indigenous culture.

Indigenous Communities and Events

Canada is a country rich in cultural diversity, with a significant Indigenous population that has contributed immensely to the nation's history and heritage. Indigenous communities in Canada have a vibrant and diverse culture, with distinct languages, traditions, art forms, and ceremonies. This travel guide aims to shed light on the incredible experiences and events that can be encountered while exploring Canada's Indigenous communities. From powwows and traditional ceremonies to art exhibits and cultural centers, travelers have the opportunity to immerse themselves in the fascinating world of Indigenous cultures.

Understanding Canada's Indigenous Communities:

1.1 Indigenous Peoples: Canada is home to three main groups of Indigenous peoples: First Nations, Inuit, and Métis. Each group has its unique cultural identity, history, and traditions.

1.2 Indigenous Languages: There are over 70 distinct Indigenous languages spoken in Canada, reflecting the linguistic diversity of these communities.

1.3 Historical Significance: It is crucial to understand the impact of colonization on Indigenous communities and the ongoing efforts to address historical injustices.

Preparing for the Journey :

2.1 Cultural Sensitivity: Respect for Indigenous traditions and customs is essential. Visitors should familiarize themselves with local protocols and customs before visiting Indigenous communities.

2.2 Traditional Territory: Acknowledging and respecting the traditional territory of Indigenous communities is a sign of respect and understanding.

Experiencing Indigenous Events and Festivals :

3.1 Powwows: Powwows are vibrant gatherings that showcase Indigenous dances, music, arts, crafts, and traditional foods. These events provide an excellent opportunity to engage with Indigenous communities and witness their cultural expressions.

3.2 Sun Dance: The Sun Dance is a sacred ceremony among many Indigenous peoples. Visitors interested in spiritual experiences can witness this significant event, which involves fasting, dancing, and prayer.

3.3 Indigenous Art Exhibits: Museums and galleries across Canada exhibit Indigenous art, including traditional crafts, contemporary paintings, sculptures, and installations. These exhibits provide insights into Indigenous history, spirituality, and artistic expressions.

3.4 Indigenous Film Festivals: Film festivals dedicated to Indigenous cinema showcase compelling stories from Indigenous filmmakers, providing a unique perspective on their experiences and cultural heritage.

3.5 National Indigenous Peoples Day: Celebrated on June 21st, National Indigenous Peoples Day is an occasion to honor and celebrate the contributions and cultures of Indigenous peoples across Canada. Festivities include traditional performances, arts and crafts, storytelling, and cultural demonstrations.

Exploring Indigenous Cultural Centers and Heritage Sites :

4.1 The Canadian Museum of History: Located in Gatineau, Quebec, this museum provides a comprehensive overview of Indigenous history, culture, and achievements in Canada.

4.2 Royal BC Museum: Situated in Victoria, British Columbia, this museum offers exhibits on First Nations' art, history, and cultural practices, including an impressive collection of totem poles.

4.3 Wanuskewin Heritage Park: Located near Saskatoon, Saskatchewan, Wanuskewin showcases the history and cultural significance of the Northern Plains Indigenous peoples, featuring archaeological sites, interpretive trails, and cultural programs.

4.4 Inuvialuit Heritage Centre: In Inuvik, Northwest Territories, visitors can explore Inuvialuit culture through exhibitions, traditional artifacts, and interactive displays, gaining insights into the unique Arctic Indigenous way of life.

Participating in Indigenous Ecotourism :

5.1 Indigenous-led Tours: Engage in eco-tours led by Indigenous guides who offer insights into their traditional knowledge, land stewardship, and conservation efforts.

5.2 Wilderness Retreats: Experience the tranquility and spirituality of the land through Indigenous-led wilderness retreats, where visitors can learn about traditional healing practices, storytelling, and survival skills.

Art and Handicrafts

Canada, known for its stunning landscapes and diverse cultural heritage, is also a treasure trove of arts and handicrafts. From intricate indigenous artworks to contemporary masterpieces, Canada offers a rich tapestry of creative expressions. This travel guide will take you on a journey through the artistic landscape of Canada, highlighting key destinations, notable artists, and traditional crafts that have shaped the country's cultural identity.

Indigenous Art:
Canada's indigenous communities have a profound artistic tradition that dates back thousands of years. The First Nations, Inuit, and Métis peoples have honed their skills in creating breathtaking artworks that reflect their spiritual beliefs, ancestral connections, and deep respect for nature. Exploring regions like British Columbia and the Canadian Arctic will provide a glimpse into the world of indigenous art, characterized by totem poles, Inuit sculptures, beadwork, and stunning cedar wood carvings.

Museums and Galleries:
Canada's major cities boast exceptional museums and galleries that showcase a wide range of artistic styles and periods. In Vancouver, the Museum of Anthropology exhibits indigenous artifacts and contemporary indigenous art, while the Vancouver Art Gallery presents both Canadian and international works. In Toronto, the Art Gallery of Ontario houses an extensive collection of Canadian art, including pieces by the iconic Group of Seven painters. Other notable institutions include the National Gallery of Canada in Ottawa and the Montreal Museum of Fine Arts.

Canadian Group of Seven:

The Group of Seven, a collective of Canadian landscape painters active from the 1920s to the 1930s, played a pivotal role in shaping Canadian art. Inspired by the country's rugged wilderness, these artists sought to capture the essence of the Canadian landscape through bold brushwork and vibrant colors. Exploring the regions that influenced the Group of Seven, such as Algoma, Georgian Bay, and Algonquin Park, allows visitors to experience the landscapes that served as their muse.

Contemporary Art Scene:

Canada's art scene is not limited to traditional forms. The country nurtures a thriving contemporary art community, with numerous art festivals, biennials, and galleries dedicated to showcasing innovative and experimental works. Cities like Montreal, Vancouver, and Toronto host dynamic art events, such as the Montreal Biennale and Nuit Blanche, offering visitors a chance to engage with cutting-edge art installations, multimedia exhibits, and performances.

Craft Traditions:

Canada's craft traditions are deeply rooted in the cultural heritage of its diverse communities. From Inuit soapstone carvings to Acadian textiles, there are numerous opportunities to explore traditional crafts across the country. The city of St. John's in Newfoundland and Labrador, for instance, is renowned for its vibrant knitting and quilting traditions, while Quebec is famous for its intricate woodwork and folk art. The Canadian Handicrafts Guild and local craft markets are excellent resources for discovering unique handmade items and interacting with local artisans.

Art Festivals and Events:
Throughout the year, Canada hosts an array of art festivals and events that celebrate creativity and cultural diversity. The Calgary Stampede in Alberta showcases indigenous art, Western art, and vibrant rodeo performances. The Stratford Festival in Ontario is a renowned theater festival that features world-class productions, while the Montreal Jazz Festival draws music enthusiasts from around the world. Attending these events offers a multifaceted experience that combines art, culture, and entertainment.

Artisan Workshops and Studios:

For those interested in a hands-on experience, Canada offers various artisan workshops and studios where visitors can learn traditional crafts or try their hand at creating their own artworks. From pottery classes in Nova Scotia to glassblowing workshops in Ontario, these interactive experiences provide a deeper understanding of the artistic process and allow travelers to take home their unique creations.

Canadian Cuisine

Canada, a land of breathtaking landscapes, vibrant cities, and rich cultural heritage, is also a haven for food enthusiasts. With its diverse population and vast geographical expanse, Canadian cuisine offers a remarkable fusion of flavors, drawing inspiration from its indigenous roots, European influences, and global culinary trends. This travel guide will delve into the delectable world of Canadian cuisine, showcasing iconic dishes, regional specialties, and must-visit food destinations across the country. Get ready to embark on a mouthwatering journey that will leave you craving for more!

Indigenous Cuisine

To truly understand Canadian cuisine, one must appreciate the indigenous culinary traditions that have shaped the country's food landscape for thousands of years. Indigenous communities across Canada, including the First Nations, Inuit, and Métis, have a deep connection with the land and its resources. Traditional dishes like bannock (a type of bread), pemmican (a dried meat and fruit mixture), and salmon cooked on cedar planks exemplify their resourcefulness and deep respect for nature. Visitors can explore indigenous food experiences through cultural festivals, indigenous-owned restaurants, and even culinary tours that offer a glimpse into traditional cooking methods and storytelling.

Atlantic Canada

The Atlantic provinces of Canada, including Newfoundland and Labrador, Prince Edward Island, Nova Scotia, and New Brunswick, boast a distinct culinary identity heavily influenced by the region's coastal geography. Seafood reigns supreme here, with lobster, scallops, oysters, and Atlantic salmon taking center stage. Don't miss out on experiencing the renowned Maritime lobster boil, a communal feast that celebrates the area's bountiful seafood. Additionally, sample traditional dishes like Jiggs' dinner (a boiled dinner with salt beef and vegetables), fish and brewis (a dish made with salt cod and hard bread), and rappie pie (a potato-based meat pie). For a unique sweet treat, try the Prince Edward Island specialty, "cow's cream" ice cream, made with fresh milk and cream from local dairy farms.

Quebec

Quebec, Canada's largest French-speaking province, is a culinary paradise blending French and North American influences. Indulge in classic French-inspired dishes like poutine, a beloved comfort food consisting of French fries smothered in cheese curds and gravy. Quebec is also famous for its exquisite maple syrup, producing over 70%

of the world's supply. Experience the sweet side of Quebec by visiting a sugar shack during maple syrup season, where you can sample maple taffy on snow and traditional dishes like tourtière (meat pie) and sugar pie. Don't forget to savor the local cheese, such as squeaky-fresh cheese curds and the renowned Oka cheese.

Ontario

The province of Ontario offers a diverse culinary scene that reflects its multicultural makeup. In the vibrant city of Toronto, known as one of the world's most multicultural cities, visitors can explore a myriad of international cuisines in its diverse neighborhoods. From dim sum in Chinatown to Indian curries in Little India, the options are endless. Niagara-on-the-Lake, located in Ontario's wine region, offers an ideal setting for indulging in wine tastings, farm-to-table dining, and culinary festivals. Ontario is also known for its iconic butter tarts, peameal bacon sandwiches, and craft beer scene, with numerous breweries scattered throughout the province.

Western Canada

The western provinces of Canada, including British Columbia, Alberta, Saskatchewan, and Manitoba, boast an abundance of natural resources, resulting in a diverse and innovative culinary scene. British Columbia's coastal location provides access to an array of fresh seafood, while Vancouver's thriving Asian community has influenced the city's vibrant sushi scene. Alberta is renowned for its beef, with world-class steakhouses and hearty Alberta beef burgers. Saskatchewan and Manitoba showcase their prairie roots with dishes like perogies (dumplings filled with potato or cheese) and wild game specialties such as bison and elk. Explore the wine regions of British Columbia's Okanagan Valley and Alberta's scenic vineyards for a taste of Canada's growing wine industry.

Regional Specialties

Canada, the second-largest country in the world, is not only known for its breathtaking landscapes but also for its diverse and mouthwatering regional specialties. From coast to coast, Canada offers a tantalizing array of culinary delights that reflect the country's multicultural heritage, natural resources, and regional influences. In this comprehensive Canada travel guide, we will take you on a gastronomic journey across the nation, exploring the unique regional specialties that make Canadian cuisine truly exceptional.

Atlantic Canada:
Located on the eastern coast, Atlantic Canada is renowned for its seafood-rich dishes and hearty comfort food. The region's proximity to the ocean allows for an abundance of fresh seafood, including succulent lobster, sweet scallops, and juicy mussels. Don't miss the famous Maritime Lobster Roll, a delectable combination of tender lobster meat, mayo, and seasonings nestled in a buttered roll. Another iconic dish is the Newfoundland Jiggs Dinner, featuring salted beef or corned beef boiled with root vegetables like potatoes, cabbage, and turnips.

Quebec:
Moving westward, the province of Quebec stands out for its unique blend of French and Canadian culinary traditions. Poutine, Quebec's beloved comfort food, is a must-try. It consists of crispy French fries smothered in rich gravy and topped with cheese curds, resulting in a decadent and satisfying dish. Another Quebec specialty is Tourtière, a savory meat pie typically filled with a combination of ground pork, beef, and spices. For

dessert, indulge in a slice of maple syrup pie or a classic French-Canadian sugar pie, known as tarte au sucre.

Ontario:

In the province of Ontario, the culinary scene is diverse, reflecting the multicultural makeup of Canada's most populous province. Toronto, the cosmopolitan capital, is a food lover's paradise, offering an eclectic range of international cuisines. However, Ontario's regional specialties also shine, such as the famous peameal bacon sandwich. This sandwich features peameal bacon, which is pork loin rolled in cornmeal, cooked until crispy, and served on a bun. Butter tarts, a sweet treat with a gooey filling made of butter, sugar, and eggs, are another Ontario delicacy.

Prairies:

Stretching across Alberta, Saskatchewan, and Manitoba, the Prairie provinces are known for their hearty and satisfying dishes. Alberta is famous for its world-class beef, so be sure to savor a perfectly grilled Alberta steak. Bison, a lean and flavorful meat, is also prominent in the region and is often featured in dishes like bison burgers or bison stew. Saskatoon berries, native to the region, are used in various desserts and jams, including the delicious Saskatoon berry pie, reminiscent of blueberries.

British Columbia:
On the western coast of Canada, British Columbia offers a diverse culinary landscape with a focus on fresh, local ingredients. The region is renowned for its seafood, particularly salmon. Try the succulent BC wild salmon, grilled to perfection or cured as lox. Another popular dish is Nanaimo bars, a no-bake dessert consisting of three layers: a chocolate-coconut base, a custard-flavored butter icing, and a glossy chocolate topping. British Columbia is also celebrated for its thriving wine industry, with vineyards dotting the picturesque landscapes of the Okanagan Valley.

Northern Canada:
Heading to the vast and remote northern regions of Canada, traditional Indigenous cuisine takes center stage. Indigenous communities have a deep connection with the land, and their cuisine incorporates ingredients like game meat, fish, wild berries, and foraged plants. Bannock, a simple and delicious bread traditionally cooked over an open fire, is a staple in Indigenous cuisine. Arctic char, a

cold-water fish, is a popular delicacy in the North and can be enjoyed smoked, pan-fried, or baked.

Food Festivals

Canada is also a haven for food enthusiasts. From coast to coast, Canadians celebrate their culinary heritage through vibrant food festivals that showcase the nation's rich gastronomic tapestry. This Canada travel guide explores some of the most prominent food festivals in the country, offering a delightful blend of flavors, traditions, and cultural experiences. So, prepare your taste buds for an epicurean adventure as we embark on a journey through Canada's diverse food festival scene.

Poutine Festivals

A quintessential Canadian dish, poutine has become an iconic symbol of the country's cuisine. Poutine festivals held in various cities, such as Montreal, Quebec City, and Ottawa, celebrate this beloved culinary creation. Visitors can indulge in endless variations of poutine, from traditional renditions featuring cheese curds and gravy to innovative twists with gourmet toppings like lobster or pulled pork. The festivals often include live music, food competitions, and entertainment, creating a lively atmosphere that perfectly complements the indulgent flavors of poutine.

Maple Syrup Festivals

Maple syrup, affectionately known as "liquid gold," holds a special place in Canadian cuisine. In spring, when the maple trees awaken, various provinces host maple syrup festivals. The most famous among them is the Sugarbush Maple Syrup Festival in Ontario, where visitors can explore maple forests, witness the syrup-making process, and savor delectable maple-infused treats. Additionally, Quebec's Cabane à Sucre (sugar shack) festivals offer a unique opportunity to indulge in traditional Québécois cuisine, including maple-glazed ham, pea soup, and tire d'érable (maple taffy) on snow.

Halifax Lobster Festival

As the lobster capital of Canada, Halifax, Nova Scotia, hosts the annual Halifax Lobster Festival. This event celebrates the region's maritime heritage and its abundant seafood offerings. Visitors can feast on succulent lobster prepared in various ways, including lobster rolls, lobster poutine, and even lobster-infused desserts. The festival also features live music, cooking demonstrations, and lobster fishing excursions, providing an immersive experience into the world of Atlantic Canadian seafood.

Icewine Festivals

In the frigid winter months, wine lovers flock to the renowned Icewine Festivals in Ontario and British Columbia. Icewine, a luscious dessert wine made from frozen grapes, is internationally acclaimed for its unique flavors. The festivals showcase an array of Icewine producers, allowing visitors to sample different vintages, learn about the winemaking process, and attend wine-pairing events. Niagara Icewine Festival and the Okanagan Winter Wine Festival offer a delightful blend of wine tastings, ice sculptures, gourmet dining, and winter activities against the backdrop of stunning winery landscapes.

Taste of Saskatchewan

The Taste of Saskatchewan festival held in Saskatoon is a culinary extravaganza featuring the province's diverse cuisine. With over 30 local restaurants participating, visitors can savor a wide range of dishes, from hearty prairie fare to international cuisines. The festival also showcases live music performances, culinary competitions, and interactive cooking demonstrations, providing a vibrant and entertaining experience for food lovers.

Canada's food festivals offer a unique way to explore the country's diverse culinary landscape while immersing oneself in local traditions and cultures. From the iconic poutine festivals to the indulgent maple syrup celebrations, each festival provides an opportunity to engage with Canadian cuisine at its finest. Whether it's savoring succulent lobster in Halifax, enjoying the sweetness of Icewine in Ontario and British Columbia, or exploring the vibrant food scene in Saskatoon, Canada's food festivals promise unforgettable gastronomic experiences. So, pack your bags, embark on a journey through the flavors of Canada, and let your taste buds indulge in the culinary delights that await you at these remarkable food festivals. Bon appétit!

Maple Syrup Experience

Canada is not only known for its breathtaking landscapes and diverse culture, but also for its deep-rooted connection with maple syrup. The maple syrup experience in Canada offers visitors a unique opportunity to immerse themselves in the rich history, traditional methods, and delightful flavors associated with this iconic Canadian treasure. From the sugaring-off season to maple syrup festivals, this travel guide will take you on a captivating journey through the enchanting world of maple syrup in Canada.

The Origins and Significance of Maple Syrup:

Maple syrup holds a special place in Canadian culture, with a history dating back centuries. Exploring the origins of maple syrup production and its significance to Indigenous communities provides valuable insights into the syrup-making process. Visitors can learn about the art of tapping maple trees, collecting sap, and the intricate process of boiling it down to create the golden elixir we all love.

The Sugaring-off Season:

The sugaring-off season, typically from late winter to early spring, is the perfect time to experience the maple syrup tradition firsthand. As the winter frost recedes, maple trees awaken, and sap begins to flow. Maple syrup producers across Canada open their doors to visitors, offering them a chance to witness the tapping process, learn about traditional tools, and indulge in mouthwatering maple-infused treats.

Maple Syrup Production:
Understanding the various methods of maple syrup production is essential to appreciating the time and effort involved in creating this sweet liquid gold. From traditional methods using spiles and buckets to modern tubing systems, visitors can explore the evolution of syrup production techniques and witness the ingenuity of Canadian maple syrup producers.

Maple Syrup Regions of Canada:
While maple syrup is produced across Canada, certain regions are particularly renowned for their maple syrup production. Exploring these regions, such as Quebec, Ontario, and New Brunswick, offers visitors a chance to delve deeper into the local maple syrup culture, taste different varieties, and

discover unique regional traditions associated with maple syrup production.

Maple Syrup Festivals:

Maple syrup festivals provide a vibrant and immersive experience for visitors. From the iconic Sugarbush Maple Syrup Festival in Ontario to the Festi-Neige in Quebec, these events showcase the best of Canadian maple syrup through guided tours, live demonstrations, tastings, and family-friendly activities. Attending a maple syrup festival is a must for anyone seeking an authentic and memorable Canadian experience.

Culinary Delights: Maple Syrup-Inspired Cuisine:

Maple syrup is not limited to pancake toppings. Its unique flavor profile lends itself to a wide range of culinary creations. Visitors can indulge in maple-infused dishes and explore the diverse ways maple syrup is incorporated into Canadian cuisine. From maple-glazed salmon to maple syrup-infused desserts, this culinary adventure is sure to leave taste buds tingling with delight.

Maple Syrup Souvenirs and Shopping:

No visit to Canada's maple syrup heartland would be complete without bringing home a taste of this beloved Canadian treat. Maple syrup-themed shops and boutiques offer an array of maple syrup products, including bottles of syrup, maple candies, maple-infused sauces, and maple sugar. These make for delightful souvenirs and gifts to share the sweetness of Canada with loved ones.

Sustainable Maple Syrup Practices:

As awareness of sustainability and environmental stewardship grows, so does the importance of responsible maple syrup production. Visitors can learn about sustainable practices employed by maple syrup producers, such as forest management, organic certification, and the use of energy-efficient technologies. Supporting producers who prioritize sustainability helps preserve the maple syrup tradition for future generations.

The maple syrup experience in Canada is a journey that combines history, tradition, taste, and natural beauty. From the enchanting sugaring-off season to vibrant maple syrup festivals, this delightful adventure offers visitors a deeper appreciation for the cultural and culinary significance of maple syrup in Canada. Whether you're a food enthusiast, nature lover, or culture seeker, immersing yourself in the maple syrup experience will create memories that are as sweet as the syrup itself.

•Arts and Entertainment

:
Canada is a country known for its stunning natural beauty, diverse landscapes, and rich cultural heritage. However, beyond its breathtaking scenery, Canada boasts a thriving arts and entertainment scene that captivates locals and visitors alike. From world-class museums and art galleries to lively festivals and captivating performances, this article will guide you through the vibrant arts and entertainment offerings across Canada, ensuring an enriching and unforgettable travel experience.

Museums and Art Galleries:
Canada is home to an impressive array of museums and art galleries that showcase both national and

international artistic treasures. In major cities like Toronto, Montreal, and Vancouver, art enthusiasts can explore renowned institutions such as the Art Gallery of Ontario, the Montreal Museum of Fine Arts, and the Vancouver Art Gallery. These institutions feature diverse collections that span various periods and artistic styles, including contemporary, indigenous, and Canadian masterpieces.

Moreover, the National Gallery of Canada in Ottawa stands as a testament to the country's commitment to preserving and celebrating its artistic heritage. Boasting an extensive collection of Canadian and international artworks, this prestigious institution hosts rotating exhibitions, providing visitors with a glimpse into the world of visual arts.

Performing Arts:

Canada's performing arts scene is a vibrant tapestry of theater, music, and dance. Cities across the country offer an array of performances, from small independent theaters to grand opera houses. In Toronto, the renowned Mirvish Theatre and the Canadian Opera Company present world-class productions, while the Stratford Festival in Ontario captivates audiences with its Shakespearean performances and contemporary plays.

Montreal, often referred to as the cultural capital of Canada, showcases its vibrant arts scene through festivals such as the Montreal Jazz Festival and the Montreal International Jazz Festival, drawing in music lovers from around the world. The city is also famous for its avant-garde theater and dance performances, with venues like Place des Arts and La Tohu offering diverse and innovative shows.

Festivals and Celebrations:
Canada is a nation that loves to celebrate, and throughout the year, a multitude of festivals and cultural events take place across the country. The Calgary Stampede, held in Alberta, is a world-renowned celebration of cowboy culture, featuring rodeos, live music, and vibrant parades. In Quebec City, the Winter Carnival brings the city to life with ice sculptures, outdoor concerts, and exhilarating winter sports activities.
For music enthusiasts, the Osheaga Music and Arts Festival in Montreal and the Calgary Folk Music Festival provide an opportunity to experience a diverse range of musical genres, performed by both Canadian and international artists.

Indigenous Arts and Culture:

Canada's indigenous communities have a rich artistic heritage that is celebrated throughout the country. Indigenous art galleries, such as the Indigenous Art Centre in Gatineau, Quebec, and the Bill Reid Gallery in Vancouver, British Columbia, showcase traditional and contemporary indigenous artwork, including paintings, sculptures, and carvings.

Moreover, attending a powwow, a traditional gathering that features ceremonial dances, music, and art, offers an authentic and immersive experience of indigenous culture. Powwows take place in various locations across Canada, providing visitors with an opportunity to witness the vibrant traditions and artistic expressions of First Nations, Métis, and Inuit peoples.

Film and Television:

Canada's film and television industry has gained international recognition for its talented actors, directors, and production crews. The Toronto International Film Festival (TIFF) stands as one of the most prominent film festivals worldwide, attracting acclaimed filmmakers and movie enthusiasts from around the globe. This festival showcases a diverse selection of films, from Hollywood blockbusters to independent productions, and serves as a platform for emerging Canadian talent.

Furthermore, cities like Vancouver and Toronto have become popular filming locations for numerous television shows and movies, with guided tours offering behind-the-scenes glimpses into the world of Canadian film and television production.

From its world-class museums and art galleries to its lively festivals and captivating performances, Canada's arts and entertainment scene is a testament to the country's rich cultural heritage and diverse artistic expressions. Whether exploring the national treasures housed in prestigious institutions or immersing oneself in the vibrant festivals and celebrations, travelers to Canada will undoubtedly be captivated by the country's artistic offerings. The vibrant tapestry of arts and entertainment in Canada promises a truly enriching and unforgettable travel experience for all who visit.

Museums and Art Galleries

Canada,From coast to coast, the country is home to numerous museums and art galleries that showcase its rich history, vibrant artistry, and diverse cultural heritage. In this comprehensive Canada travel guide, we will delve into some of the most noteworthy museums and art galleries across the country, providing you with an insight into the captivating world of Canadian art, history, and culture.

National Gallery of Canada - Ottawa, Ontario:

Located in the heart of Canada's capital, the National Gallery of Canada is a premier destination for art enthusiasts. Housing an extensive collection of Canadian and international art, the gallery showcases works ranging from classic to contemporary. Visitors can admire iconic pieces like the Group of Seven's landscape paintings and Emily Carr's distinctive portrayals of British Columbia. The National Gallery also hosts temporary exhibitions, educational programs, and guided tours, making it a must-visit for art lovers of all ages.

Royal Ontario Museum - Toronto, Ontario:

The Royal Ontario Museum (ROM) is Canada's largest museum of world cultures and natural history. With a diverse collection of over six million artifacts, the ROM offers a fascinating journey through time and across continents. Visitors can explore ancient Egyptian mummies, marvel at dinosaur skeletons, and delve into interactive exhibits that showcase the cultural heritage of various civilizations. The ROM also features rotating exhibitions, including contemporary art installations, making it a captivating destination for both history buffs and art enthusiasts.

Musée des beaux-arts de Montréal - Montreal, Quebec:

Situated in the vibrant city of Montreal, the Musée des beaux-arts de Montréal (Montreal Museum of Fine Arts) is renowned for its comprehensive collection spanning various artistic periods and styles. The museum boasts an extensive assortment of Canadian and international art, including works by renowned artists such as Rembrandt, Picasso, and Warhol. In addition to its permanent collection, the museum regularly hosts temporary exhibitions, musical performances, and educational programs, making it a cultural hub that offers something for everyone.

Canadian Museum of History - Gatineau, Quebec:

Located just across the river from Ottawa, the Canadian Museum of History showcases the rich heritage and diverse stories of Canada and its people. Through captivating exhibits, multimedia presentations, and interactive displays, visitors can explore the country's history, from its Indigenous roots to contemporary times. The museum's renowned Grand Hall houses the world's largest indoor collection of totem poles, while other galleries highlight important events, cultural traditions, and contributions of various communities that have shaped the nation.

Art Gallery of Ontario - Toronto, Ontario:

The Art Gallery of Ontario (AGO) is one of the largest art museums in North America, renowned for its extensive collection of Canadian, European, African, and contemporary art. The AGO houses more than 95,000 works, including pieces by Canadian artists like Tom Thomson and the Group of Seven, as well as European masters such as Monet, Van Gogh, and Rubens. The museum also features dynamic exhibitions, art workshops, and film screenings, offering a vibrant cultural experience for visitors of all backgrounds.

Museum of Anthropology - Vancouver, British Columbia:

Nestled on the campus of the University of British Columbia, the Museum of Anthropology (MOA) showcases the rich Indigenous cultures of British Columbia and beyond. The museum's striking architecture, designed by renowned architect Arthur Erickson, harmoniously integrates with its surroundings, creating a captivating atmosphere. Inside, visitors can admire a vast collection of Indigenous art, including intricately carved totem poles, masks, and other artifacts that highlight the region's cultural diversity. The MOA also hosts cultural events, storytelling sessions, and workshops, providing visitors with a deeper understanding of Indigenous traditions and contemporary issues.

The Rooms - St. John's, Newfoundland and Labrador:

The Rooms is a cultural facility in St. John's, Newfoundland and Labrador, that combines an art gallery, a museum, and an archives. The gallery showcases an impressive collection of visual art, highlighting the unique artistic expressions of Newfoundland and Labrador. The museum offers exhibits that delve into the province's natural history, cultural heritage, and diverse communities. The Rooms also serves as a hub for cultural activities, hosting performances, concerts, and literary events that celebrate the province's artistic talent and vibrant traditions.

Music and Theater

Canada offers a vibrant and thriving music and theater scene. From the enchanting symphonies performed in concert halls to the spellbinding dramas showcased on stage, this vast country is a haven for music and theater enthusiasts. In this comprehensive travel guide, we will delve into the rich tapestry of Canada's music and theater landscape, highlighting key cities, renowned venues, festivals, and notable artists that have shaped and continue to shape the nation's artistic identity.

A Symphony of Sounds:
1.1. Toronto: The Musical Capital

1.2. Montreal: Where Music Meets Passion
1.3. Vancouver: A Melodic Pacific Oasis
1.4. Ottawa: The Capital of Harmonies

The Enchanting World of Theater:
2.1. Stratford: Shakespearean Grandeur
2.2. Toronto: Broadway North
2.3. Montreal: Francophone Theater Hub
2.4. Calgary: A Dynamic Theater Scene

Festivals Celebrating Artistic Brilliance:
3.1. Toronto International Film Festival (TIFF)
3.2. Montreal International Jazz Festival
3.3. Stratford Festival
3.4. Edmonton International Fringe Festival

Notable Artists and Productions:
4.1. Joni Mitchell: The Voice of a Generation
4.2. Cirque du Soleil: A Mesmerizing Theatrical Spectacle
4.3. The Tragically Hip: A Canadian Rock Legacy
4.4. Robert Lepage: Master of Visual Theater

Music and Theater Education:
5.1. National Theatre School of Canada
5.2. Royal Conservatory of Music
5.3. Berklee College of Music - Valencia Campus

As you embark on your journey through Canada, make sure to immerse yourself in the country's rich music and theater culture. From the bustling streets of Toronto to the charming theaters of Stratford, you will find a plethora of performances that captivate your senses and leave lasting impressions. Whether you are an ardent fan of classical symphonies, modern dramas, or experimental productions, Canada's music and theater scene promises to deliver a diverse range of experiences. So, don't miss the opportunity to witness the magic unfold on stages and in concert halls across the nation, and let the melodies and dramas of Canada inspire your soul.

Film Festivals

Canada also boasts a thriving film festival scene. From coast to coast, the country hosts numerous internationally acclaimed film festivals that attract both domestic and international filmmakers, industry professionals, and movie enthusiasts. In this comprehensive travel guide, we will delve into the exciting world of film festivals in Canada, highlighting the major events, exploring the diverse range of cinematic offerings, and providing practical information for travelers interested in attending these cultural celebrations.

Toronto International Film Festival (TIFF) : Undoubtedly the most prestigious film festival in Canada, the Toronto International Film Festival (TIFF) takes place annually in September. Regarded as a leading platform for both Hollywood and independent films, TIFF showcases a vast array of genres, including feature films, documentaries, and short films. The festival draws renowned filmmakers, actors, and industry professionals from around the world, creating a dynamic atmosphere buzzing with creative energy. Visitors can enjoy screenings at various venues throughout the city, attend industry events, and engage in Q&A sessions with filmmakers and actors. TIFF serves as an ideal launching pad for films aiming to secure global distribution, and attendees often witness the premiere of highly anticipated movies.

Vancouver International Film Festival (VIFF) :

Located on the picturesque west coast, the Vancouver International Film Festival (VIFF) celebrates the art of filmmaking from around the globe. Held annually in September and October, VIFF showcases an eclectic mix of international and Canadian films, embracing diverse cultures and perspectives. The festival features a wide range of genres, including arthouse cinema, documentaries, and Indigenous films, appealing to a broad audience. In addition to film screenings, VIFF hosts industry events, panel discussions, and workshops, providing a platform for networking and fostering creative exchange. Vancouver's vibrant cityscape and natural beauty serve as a stunning backdrop for this engaging cinematic experience.

Festival du Nouveau Cinéma (FNC) - Montreal :

As one of the oldest film festivals in Canada, the Festival du Nouveau Cinéma (FNC) in Montreal showcases cutting-edge and innovative cinema. Held annually in October, FNC focuses on highlighting emerging talents and experimental works from both Canadian and international filmmakers. The festival's program includes feature films, shorts, virtual reality experiences, and interactive installations, pushing the boundaries of traditional storytelling. FNC also incorporates live performances, exhibitions, and conferences, creating a multi-disciplinary environment that engages audiences in unique and thought-provoking ways. The vibrant city of Montreal, with its rich cultural heritage and thriving arts scene, provides an ideal backdrop for this avant-garde celebration of cinema.

Atlantic International Film Festival (AIFF) - Halifax :

Nestled on the stunning Atlantic coast, the Atlantic International Film Festival (AIFF) in Halifax, Nova Scotia, celebrates the talent and creativity of filmmakers from the Atlantic region and beyond. Taking place annually in September, AIFF showcases a diverse selection of films, ranging from local independent productions to international releases. The festival provides a platform for emerging talent, giving them an opportunity to showcase their work to a wider audience. Visitors can immerse themselves in the vibrant maritime atmosphere, attend screenings and events, and engage in conversations with filmmakers. AIFF also offers industry-focused sessions, workshops, and networking opportunities, making it a valuable destination for both film enthusiasts and industry professionals.

Calgary International Film Festival (CIFF) :

The Calgary International Film Festival (CIFF), held annually in September, has become a prominent cultural event in Western Canada. CIFF presents an extensive program of feature films, documentaries, and shorts from around the world, aiming to captivate diverse audiences. The festival focuses on promoting Canadian cinema while also celebrating international films that reflect global perspectives. CIFF features unique thematic strands, such as environmental sustainability and LGBTQ+ narratives, showcasing a diverse range of voices and stories. Alongside film screenings, CIFF offers industry events, panel discussions, and interactive experiences, creating a vibrant atmosphere for filmmakers, industry professionals, and moviegoers alike. Calgary's cosmopolitan charm, coupled with its stunning natural surroundings, makes it an enticing destination for film enthusiasts.

Canada's film festival scene offers a captivating blend of diverse cinematic experiences, from the glamorous red carpets of Toronto to the avant-garde experiments in Montreal and the coastal celebrations in Halifax and Vancouver. These festivals provide a platform for filmmakers to showcase their work, foster creative exchange, and engage with audiences from different backgrounds. Attending these cultural events not only offers a chance to explore the world of cinema but also provides an opportunity to immerse oneself in the unique cultural fabric of each host city. Whether you're an ardent film buff, an aspiring filmmaker, or a traveler seeking new cultural experiences, Canada's film festivals offer an enchanting journey into the world of storytelling and creativity.

Chapter Six

Outdoor Adventures

•Hiking and Camping

Canada's vast and diverse landscapes make it a paradise for outdoor enthusiasts. With its sprawling national parks, stunning mountains, pristine lakes, and dense forests, Canada offers endless opportunities for hiking and camping adventures. This comprehensive travel guide aims to provide you with essential information and recommendations to make the most of your hiking and camping experiences in Canada.

I. Planning Your Trip:

Choosing the Right Time:

Canada experiences distinct seasons, and the best time for hiking and camping varies depending on the region.
Summer (June to August) offers mild temperatures and longer days, making it ideal for most outdoor activities.

Spring (April to June) and fall (September to October) provide pleasant weather and stunning foliage, but conditions can be unpredictable.
Winter (November to March) is suitable for winter sports enthusiasts but requires specialized gear and experience.
Selecting a Destination:

Canada boasts numerous national parks, each offering unique landscapes and hiking opportunities.
Banff National Park (Alberta), Jasper National Park (Alberta), and Pacific Rim National Park Reserve (British Columbia) are popular choices.
Consider factors like accessibility, trail difficulty, and specific features such as mountains, lakes, or wildlife.
Researching and Obtaining Permits:

Some parks require permits or reservations for camping and specific hiking trails.
Check the park's official website for up-to-date information, permit availability, and any restrictions.
Book campsites and obtain permits well in advance, especially during peak season.

II. Essential Gear and Safety:

Hiking Gear:

Invest in sturdy and comfortable hiking boots, moisture-wicking clothing, and layers for variable weather conditions.
Carry a backpack with essentials like a map, compass, water bottles, high-energy snacks, a first aid kit, a headlamp, and a multi-tool.
Camping Gear:

Choose a suitable tent, sleeping bag, sleeping pad, and camping stove based on your preferences and the expected weather conditions.
Pack lightweight, nutritious food, a water filtration system, cooking utensils, insect repellent, sunscreen, and toiletries.
Safety Measures:

Inform someone about your hiking and camping plans, including your expected return date.
Familiarize yourself with the park's rules, regulations, and safety guidelines.
Be aware of wildlife encounters and practice proper food storage techniques.
Carry a bear spray and know how to use it.

Check weather forecasts regularly and be prepared for sudden changes.

III. Hiking and Camping in Canada:

Popular Hiking Trails:

West Coast Trail (British Columbia): A challenging coastal hike renowned for its rugged beauty and stunning ocean views.
Bruce Trail (Ontario): Canada's oldest and longest marked footpath, offering diverse landscapes and unique geological features.
Gros Morne National Park (Newfoundland and Labrador): Home to the challenging Long Range Traverse, showcasing breathtaking fjords and peaks.
Camping in National Parks:

Most national parks offer a variety of camping options, including frontcountry, backcountry, and wilderness camping.
Frontcountry camping provides amenities like fire pits, picnic tables, and restrooms, while backcountry camping offers a more remote experience.

Research each park's camping regulations, reservation systems, and any specific guidelines regarding food storage and campfires.
Leave No Trace Principles:

Practice the Leave No Trace principles to minimize your impact on the environment.
Respect wildlife, stay on designated trails, pack out all trash, and use established campsites.
Follow guidelines for waste disposal, including human waste, to maintain the pristine nature of Canada's wilderness.

IV. Unique Experiences in Canada:

Coastal Hiking:

Explore the rugged beauty of Canada's coastlines, including the West Coast Trail (British Columbia) and the East Coast Trail (Newfoundland and Labrador).
Marvel at stunning sea stacks, hidden coves, and abundant marine life along these scenic trails.
Mountain Adventures:

Embark on thrilling alpine hikes in the Canadian Rockies, including the famous Sunshine Meadows (Alberta) or Wilcox Pass (Alberta).
Consider challenging yourself with a summit attempt on iconic peaks like Mount Assiniboine (British Columbia) or Mount Temple (Alberta).
Wildlife Encounters:

Canada is home to a diverse array of wildlife, including bears, moose, wolves, and eagles. Research specific parks known for wildlife sightings, such as Riding Mountain National Park (Manitoba) or Algonquin Provincial Park (Ontario). Exercise caution and maintain a safe distance when observing wildlife in their natural habitats.
Conclusion:

Hiking and camping in Canada provide unparalleled opportunities to immerse oneself in the country's breathtaking natural beauty. With careful planning, essential gear, and a focus on safety and sustainability, you can create unforgettable experiences in Canada's national parks and wilderness areas. So, pack your bags, lace up your boots, and embark on a journey to discover the wonders of hiking and camping in the Great White North.

National and Provincial Parks

Canada, is renowned for its breathtaking natural landscapes and pristine wilderness, boasting an extensive network of national and provincial parks. From towering mountains and cascading waterfalls to ancient forests and expansive coastlines, these protected areas offer a paradise for outdoor enthusiasts, wildlife lovers, and adventure seekers. In this comprehensive travel guide, we will delve into the diverse range of national and provincial parks across Canada, highlighting their unique features, activities, and attractions. Whether you seek serenity, thrilling adventures, or a chance to immerse yourself in nature's beauty, Canada's parks are waiting to be explored.

I. National Parks:

Banff National Park:

Location: Alberta
Highlights: Majestic Rocky Mountains, turquoise lakes (e.g., Lake Louise, Moraine Lake), stunning glaciers (e.g., Columbia Icefield), hot springs (e.g., Banff Upper Hot Springs), and iconic wildlife (e.g., grizzly bears, elk).
Activities: Hiking, camping, wildlife spotting, scenic drives, skiing, snowboarding, and photography.
Must-Visit Attractions: Banff Townsite, Johnston Canyon, Sunshine Village, and the Banff Park Museum.
Jasper National Park:

Location: Alberta
Highlights: Rugged mountain peaks (e.g., Mount Edith Cavell), impressive glaciers (e.g., Athabasca Glacier), sparkling lakes (e.g., Maligne Lake), and abundant wildlife (e.g., bighorn sheep, moose).
Activities: Hiking, wildlife safaris, whitewater rafting, kayaking, fishing, skiing, and stargazing.
Must-Visit Attractions: Maligne Canyon, Spirit Island, Athabasca Falls, and the Columbia Icefield.
Gros Morne National Park:

Location: Newfoundland and Labrador

Highlights: Spectacular fjords (e.g., Western Brook Pond), ancient mountains (e.g., Tablelands), diverse ecosystems, and unique geology.
Activities: Hiking, boat tours, wildlife viewing, camping, birdwatching, and exploring coastal communities.
Must-Visit Attractions: Gros Morne Mountain, Green Gardens Trail, Lobster Cove Head Lighthouse, and Norris Point.
Pacific Rim National Park Reserve:

Location: British Columbia
Highlights: Rugged coastline, sandy beaches, old-growth rainforests, and abundant marine life.
Activities: Surfing, kayaking, beachcombing, hiking, wildlife watching, storm watching, and camping.
Must-Visit Attractions: Long Beach, Broken Group Islands, Rainforest Trail, and the Kwisitis Visitor Centre.

II. Provincial Parks:

Algonquin Provincial Park:

Location: Ontario

Highlights: Vast forests, over 2,400 lakes, picturesque rivers, and diverse wildlife (e.g., moose, wolves, loons).

Activities: Canoeing, kayaking, fishing, camping, hiking, wildlife photography, and cross-country skiing.

Must-Visit Attractions: Highway 60 Corridor, Algonquin Logging Museum, Barron Canyon Trail, and the Visitor Centre.

Fundy National Park:

Location: New Brunswick

Highlights: Dramatic tides (highest in the world), rugged coastline, ancient forests, and diverse bird species.

Activities: Hiking, camping, kayaking, beachcombing, wildlife spotting, golfing, and photography.

Must-Visit Attractions: Hopewell Rocks, Dickson Falls Trail, Alma Village, and the Fundy Trail Parkway.

Kluane National Park and Reserve:

Location: Yukon

Highlights: Towering peaks (e.g., Mount Logan), icefields, glaciers, and abundant wildlife (e.g., Dall sheep, grizzly bears).

Activities: Mountaineering, hiking, wildlife viewing, fishing, river rafting, and flightseeing.
Must-Visit Attractions: Lowell Glacier, Kathleen Lake, Mush Lake Road, and the Da Kų Cultural Centre.
Cape Breton Highlands National Park:

Location: Nova Scotia
Highlights: Scenic coastal drives (e.g., Cabot Trail), rugged cliffs, vibrant fall colors, and diverse wildlife.
Activities: Hiking, camping, whale watching, birding, golfing, cycling, and photography.
Must-Visit Attractions: Skyline Trail, Lone Shieling, Middle Head Trail, and the Chéticamp Visitor Centre.

III. Tips for Park Visitors:

Park Regulations and Permits:

Understand park rules and regulations.
Check for any permits required for activities such as camping, fishing, or backcountry exploration.
Safety Precautions:

Research and prepare for the specific challenges of each park.
Carry appropriate gear, including maps, first aid kits, and bear spray.
Inform someone about your itinerary and expected return time.
Wildlife Etiquette:

Respect wildlife and maintain a safe distance.
Do not feed or approach animals.
Properly store food to avoid attracting wildlife.
Leave No Trace:

Follow the principles of Leave No Trace ethics.
Pack out all trash and dispose of it properly.
Minimize impact on natural surroundings.

Canada's national and provincial parks provide an unrivaled opportunity to experience the country's natural wonders. This travel guide has introduced you to a selection of remarkable parks across the country, each offering its own unique features and activities. Whether you're seeking adventure, tranquility, or a chance to connect

Coastal Trails

Canada's vast coastline stretches over 202,080 kilometers, offering a treasure trove of awe-inspiring natural beauty. This guide invites you to embark on an unforgettable journey along Canada's coastal trails. From the rugged cliffs of Newfoundland and Labrador to the pristine beaches of British Columbia, each trail presents a unique blend of breathtaking landscapes, diverse wildlife, and rich cultural heritage. Immerse yourself in the tranquility of the coastal regions, where the rhythmic sound of crashing waves and the crisp ocean breeze create an invigorating atmosphere. Discover the best coastal trails Canada has to offer and prepare to be captivated by the country's stunning coastal wonders.

Newfoundland and Labrador

The easternmost province of Canada boasts a dramatic coastline and a plethora of exhilarating trails. Explore the East Coast Trail, a 336-kilometer network of paths that winds through towering cliffs, hidden coves, and charming fishing villages. Marvel at the panoramic views of the Atlantic Ocean and spot puffins, whales, and icebergs along the way. Signal Hill National Historic Site near St. John's offers a shorter but equally scenic trail, leading to Cabot Tower and providing breathtaking vistas of the city and coastline. For a unique experience, venture to Gros Morne National Park, a UNESCO World Heritage Site, where you can hike along rugged fjords, through dense forests, and up stunning mountain ranges.

Nova Scotia

In Nova Scotia, coastal trails offer a blend of history, culture, and natural beauty. Explore Cape Breton Island's Cabot Trail, a 298-kilometer loop that winds through the Cape Breton Highlands National Park. This iconic trail offers breathtaking ocean views, lush forests, and opportunities for wildlife spotting. Don't miss the stunning Peggy's Cove, a picturesque fishing village renowned for its lighthouse and granite rock formations. The coastline also offers the stunning Kejimkujik National Park and National Historic Site, where you can explore over 60 kilometers of trails, showcasing diverse ecosystems and Mi'kmaq heritage.

New Brunswick

New Brunswick's coastline is known for its rugged beauty and charming coastal villages. Experience the Fundy Trail Parkway, a 19-kilometer drive with numerous trails and lookout points that provide breathtaking views of the Bay of Fundy. Witness the world's highest tides and explore secluded beaches, dramatic cliffs, and pristine forests. Hopewell Rocks, a unique formation shaped by the tides, offers a memorable coastal hiking experience. Kouchibouguac National Park boasts over 60 kilometers of trails, weaving through salt marshes, sand dunes, and Acadian forests.

Prince Edward Island

Prince Edward Island's coastal trails offer a tranquil escape with stunning vistas and a rich cultural heritage. The Confederation Trail, once a railway line, is now a 470-kilometer multi-use trail that takes you through charming communities, farmland, and scenic coastlines. Along the way, discover lighthouses, picturesque beaches, and delicious seafood. Don't miss Prince Edward Island National Park, where you can explore stunning sandy beaches, windswept dunes, and enchanting forest trails.

British Columbia

British Columbia's coastal trails boast breathtaking landscapes, ancient rainforests, and diverse wildlife. The West Coast Trail, one of Canada's most challenging hikes, stretches for 75 kilometers through Pacific Rim National Park Reserve. This epic trail offers a thrilling experience along rugged cliffs, sandy beaches, and through lush rainforests. For a more leisurely option, the Juan de Fuca Marine Trail provides 47 kilometers of stunning coastal scenery and wildlife encounters. The Sunshine Coast Trail, the longest hut-to-hut hiking trail in Canada, stretches over 180 kilometers, offering a unique backcountry experience through lush forests and mountain vistas.

Canada's coastal trails are a nature lover's paradise, providing an unforgettable opportunity to explore the country's diverse coastal regions. From the remote cliffs of Newfoundland and Labrador to the pristine beaches of British Columbia, each trail offers a unique blend of natural wonders, cultural heritage, and stunning vistas. Whether you seek adventure or tranquility, Canada's coastal trails will captivate your senses and leave you with cherished memories. Remember to check local regulations, pack appropriately, and respect the pristine environment. Embark on your coastal trail adventure in Canada and prepare to be enchanted by the beauty that awaits at every turn.

Mountain Hikes

Canada, the land of breathtaking landscapes and diverse natural wonders, is a hiker's paradise. With its vast wilderness and towering mountain ranges, it offers countless opportunities for unforgettable hiking adventures. This comprehensive travel guide delves into the mesmerizing world of mountain hikes in Canada, presenting a curated selection of awe-inspiring trails that will captivate nature enthusiasts and outdoor adventurers alike. From the towering peaks of the Canadian Rockies to the rugged charm of the Coastal Mountains, Canada offers an array of hiking experiences that cater to all skill levels. So, lace up your hiking boots and prepare to explore the untamed beauty of Canada's mountainous terrains.

Canadian Rockies

The Canadian Rockies, located primarily in Alberta and British Columbia, are an epitome of natural grandeur. This region boasts an extensive network of trails that traverse through lush valleys, turquoise lakes, and snow-capped peaks. Banff National Park, the crown jewel of the Rockies, is home to iconic hikes such as the Banff Sunshine Meadows, Sentinel Pass, and Plain of Six Glaciers. Jasper National Park, another gem in the Rockies, presents opportunities to hike along the majestic Columbia Icefield, explore the Maligne Canyon, and summit the famous Mount Edith Cavell. Yoho National Park offers captivating hikes to the stunning Lake O'Hara and the mesmerizing Takakkaw Falls. These hikes showcase the pristine beauty of the Canadian Rockies and provide a glimpse into the region's rich wildlife and geological wonders.

Coastal Mountains

Stretching along the western edge of British Columbia, the Coastal Mountains are a rugged and awe-inspiring range that merges with the Pacific Ocean. Known for their lush rainforests, towering peaks, and picturesque fjords, this region offers unique hiking opportunities. The West Coast Trail on Vancouver Island is a world-renowned trek that traverses through lush forests, rugged coastline, and pristine beaches. For a shorter but equally rewarding hike, the Stawamus Chief in Squamish provides panoramic views of the Howe Sound and surrounding mountains. Further north, the Sunshine Coast Trail offers a stunning 180-kilometer journey through diverse landscapes, including old-growth forests, tranquil lakes, and cascading waterfalls. The Coastal Mountains provide an opportunity to immerse yourself in the wild beauty of the Pacific Northwest.

Canadian Maritimes

Beyond the towering peaks of the west, the Canadian Maritimes offer a distinct charm and an array of unique hiking experiences. Cape Breton Highlands National Park in Nova Scotia is a hiker's delight, with its renowned Cabot Trail offering spectacular coastal vistas and encounters with the renowned Cape Breton hospitality. Gros Morne National Park in Newfoundland and Labrador is a UNESCO World Heritage site, featuring the iconic Gros Morne Mountain and the Tablelands, showcasing the Earth's mantle exposed to the surface. The Fundy National Park in New Brunswick boasts the Fundy Footpath, a challenging coastal hike that offers dramatic views of the world's highest tides. The Maritimes blend stunning coastal scenery, vibrant culture, and warm hospitality to create a hiking experience like no other.

Canadian Arctic

For the adventurous souls seeking truly off-the-beaten-path hiking experiences, the Canadian Arctic beckons. Auyuittuq National Park on Baffin Island offers a thrilling expedition amidst towering peaks, massive glaciers, and vast Arctic tundra. The rugged and remote Torngat Mountains National Park in Newfoundland and Labrador is a sacred land of fjords, polar bears, and ancient Inuit culture, providing a truly unforgettable wilderness adventure. These Arctic destinations require careful planning, specialized gear, and experience in remote wilderness travel, but the rewards are immeasurable for those seeking extraordinary and untouched landscapes.

•Wildlife Viewing

Canada is renowned for its diverse and abundant wildlife, making it a prime destination for wildlife viewing enthusiasts. From the majestic polar bears of the Arctic to the elusive cougars of the Rocky Mountains, Canada offers a wide array of unique and captivating animal species.

One of the most iconic wildlife viewing experiences in Canada is observing the polar bears in Churchill, Manitoba. Located on the edge of Hudson Bay, Churchill is known as the "Polar Bear Capital of the World." Every fall, polar bears migrate to the area, waiting for the sea ice to form. Travelers can embark on guided tours and witness these magnificent creatures up close in their natural habitat, either by boat or on specially designed tundra buggies.

For those interested in marine wildlife, a visit to the coastal regions of British Columbia is a must. The Great Bear Rainforest, located on the central coast of British Columbia, is home to grizzly bears, black bears, whales, sea lions, and countless bird species. Visitors can embark on boat tours or kayak expeditions to observe these creatures in their pristine environment, while also immersing themselves in the breathtaking beauty of the coastal rainforest.

The Canadian Rockies also offer excellent opportunities for wildlife viewing. In places like Banff and Jasper National Parks, visitors can encounter a variety of species such as elk, moose, bighorn sheep, and mountain goats. These parks provide numerous hiking trails and scenic drives, allowing visitors to explore the stunning landscapes while keeping an eye out for wildlife.

Birdwatching enthusiasts will find Canada to be a haven. The country boasts a wide range of bird species, including bald eagles, puffins, loons, and numerous migratory birds. Important birding areas like Point Pelee National Park in Ontario and Prince Edward Island's Gulf Shore offer exceptional opportunities to observe and photograph a diverse array of avian species.

Bear Watching

Canada offers an unparalleled opportunity for bear watching. With its breathtaking landscapes and abundant wildlife , Canada attracts nature enthusiasts from around the world. From the rugged mountains of British Columbia to the coastal regions of Newfoundland and Labrador, this guide will take you on an unforgettable journey through some of the best bear watching destinations in Canada. So, pack your binoculars and let's embark on an adventure to witness these magnificent creatures in their natural habitat.

Grizzly Bears in British Columbia:
One of the prime bear watching destinations in Canada is British Columbia, home to the mighty Grizzly bear. The Great Bear Rainforest, located on the central and northern coast of British Columbia, is a haven for these incredible creatures. Tour operators offer guided tours, allowing visitors to observe Grizzly bears from a safe distance. The Khutzeymateen Grizzly Bear Sanctuary, a protected area north of Prince Rupert, offers a unique opportunity to view these majestic animals up close.

Polar Bears in Churchill, Manitoba:
Churchill, Manitoba, is widely recognized as the "Polar Bear Capital of the World." Every fall, as the ice forms on Hudson Bay, hundreds of polar bears gather near Churchill, waiting for the winter freeze to embark on their hunting expeditions. Specialized tours, such as tundra buggy safaris and guided walks, provide visitors with a chance to witness

these incredible predators in their natural habitat. Along with polar bears, you may also encounter other Arctic wildlife, including Arctic foxes and snowy owls.

Black Bears in Vancouver Island, British Columbia:

Vancouver Island, off the coast of British Columbia, is renowned for its abundant black bear population. The island's dense forests and pristine wilderness create the perfect habitat for these iconic bears. Guided tours take visitors on excursions through the island's coastal rainforests, where they can observe black bears foraging for food, climbing trees, and interacting with their young. The Great Bear Rainforest on the island is also home to the elusive white Kermode bear, also known as the "spirit bear."

Spirit Bears in the Great Bear Rainforest:

The Great Bear Rainforest, stretching along the central and northern coast of British Columbia, is not only home to grizzly bears and black bears but also houses a rare subspecies known as the spirit bear or Kermode bear. These unique bears, with their cream-colored fur, are found almost exclusively in this region. Witnessing a spirit bear in its natural habitat is a truly once-in-a-lifetime experience. Local tour operators provide knowledgeable guides who can lead you through this pristine wilderness, increasing your chances of spotting these elusive creatures.

Black Bears in Algonquin Provincial Park, Ontario:

Algonquin Provincial Park, located in Ontario, is one of Canada's oldest and most iconic parks, famous for its black bear population. This sprawling park offers a variety of trails and camping opportunities, allowing visitors to immerse themselves in the beauty of the Canadian wilderness. Guided tours and wildlife interpretation programs offer insights into the behavior and ecology of black bears while ensuring a safe and respectful experience for both bears and visitors.

Brown Bears in Gwaii Haanas National Park Reserve, British Columbia:

Gwaii Haanas National Park Reserve, located in the Haida Gwaii archipelago of British Columbia, is a remote and untouched wilderness that is home to a thriving population of brown bears. Accessible only by boat or seaplane, this park offers an intimate and authentic bear watching experience. Guided tours allow visitors to explore the pristine forests and coastal regions, witnessing brown bears fishing for salmon in the streams and rivers.

Bird Watching

Canada is a paradise for bird enthusiasts, offering diverse habitats and a rich avian population. From coast to coast, this vast country boasts an incredible variety of bird species, attracting birdwatchers from around the globe. Whether you are a seasoned birder or a novice looking to embark on an unforgettable avian adventure, this comprehensive travel guide will provide you with valuable information and insights into bird watching in Canada.

Biodiversity and Habitats:
Canada's vast size and diverse landscapes contribute to its incredible biodiversity, making it a haven for birdlife. The country's geographical regions, including the Arctic tundra, boreal forests, coastal marshes, prairies, and mountains, offer a wide range of habitats that support a remarkable variety of bird species. This section will explore

some of the key regions and their unique avian ecosystems.

a) Boreal Forests: Stretching across Canada's northern regions, the boreal forests are home to a multitude of bird species, including the iconic loons, owls, warblers, and woodpeckers. Exploring these remote wilderness areas can provide opportunities to witness rare and elusive birds.

b) Coastal Areas: Canada's extensive coastline provides critical nesting and feeding grounds for countless seabirds, such as puffins, gulls, and terns. The Atlantic and Pacific shores offer breathtaking opportunities for observing marine bird colonies.

c) Grasslands and Prairies: The prairies of Canada's central regions are characterized by vast grasslands, attracting a variety of raptors, including hawks, eagles, and falcons. Additionally, species like prairie chickens, sparrows, and meadowlarks can be found here.

d) Wetlands and Marshes: Canada's wetlands and marshes serve as important stopover points for migratory birds. These areas offer fantastic opportunities to observe waterfowl, herons, egrets, and many other species. Renowned wetlands, such as the Quill Lakes in Saskatchewan and Point Pelee National Park in Ontario, are must-visit destinations for birders.

Seasonal Bird Migration:

Canada's strategic location along major migratory flyways makes it a prime destination for bird watchers during the spring and fall migration seasons. Millions of birds travel through Canada each year, undertaking long journeys between their breeding and wintering grounds. Understanding the patterns and timing of bird migration is crucial for planning a successful birding trip. This section will delve into the key migration routes, timing, and prime locations to witness these impressive avian spectacles.

a) Atlantic Flyway: The Atlantic coast of Canada witnesses a spectacular passage of migratory birds, including shorebirds, waterfowl, and songbirds. Prominent hotspots along this flyway include Newfoundland and Labrador, Prince Edward Island, and the Bay of Fundy in New Brunswick.

b) Pacific Flyway: British Columbia's coastal areas serve as crucial stopovers for birds migrating along the Pacific Flyway. Vancouver Island, the Fraser River Delta, and the Great Bear Rainforest are renowned for their diverse avifauna during the migration season.

c) Central Flyway: The interior of Canada, particularly the Prairie Provinces, experiences a significant influx of migratory birds during spring and fall. The Quill Lakes in Saskatchewan and the boreal forests of Manitoba are notable locations for observing these annual movements.

Iconic Bird Species:

Canada is home to several iconic bird species that capture the imagination of bird watchers worldwide. This section will highlight some of the most sought-after species and the regions where they can be found.

a) Bald Eagle: This majestic bird of prey can be spotted in coastal regions and near large bodies of water throughout Canada. Areas like Haida Gwaii in British Columbia and the Bay of Fundy in Nova Scotia provide excellent opportunities for eagle sightings.

b) Puffin: These adorable seabirds nest in large colonies along the Atlantic coast, particularly in Newfoundland and Labrador. Bird lovers can witness their comical behaviors and vibrant beaks during breeding season.

c) Whooping Crane: With only a few hundred remaining in the wild, the whooping crane is one of North America's most endangered species. Wood Buffalo National Park in Alberta and Aransas National Wildlife Refuge in Texas serve as key breeding and wintering grounds for this magnificent bird.

Birding Hotspots and Nature Reserves:
Canada boasts an extensive network of national parks, nature reserves, and bird sanctuaries that provide protected habitats for a wide array of bird species. This section will feature some of the most renowned birding hotspots and provide insights into their unique offerings.
a) Point Pelee National Park, Ontario: Known as the "Warbler Capital of North America," this park attracts bird watchers with its impressive variety of migrating warblers and other songbirds.

b) Algonquin Provincial Park, Ontario: Located in the heart of Ontario's boreal forest, this park is a haven for birders, offering opportunities to spot loons, owls, and boreal specialties like the black-backed woodpecker.

c) Churchill, Manitoba: Famous for its polar bears, Churchill is also a prime location for birding. The area is known for its raptors, shorebirds, and the chance to witness the remarkable spectacle of snowy owls in the winter.

d) Prince Edward Island National Park: This picturesque island is a paradise for bird enthusiasts, providing habitats for migratory shorebirds, waterfowl, and a thriving population of the endangered piping plover.

Bird Watching Tips and Etiquette:
To maximize your bird watching experience and minimize disturbances to avian habitats, it is essential to follow proper birding etiquette. This section will offer practical tips for birders, including equipment suggestions, field identification techniques, ethical considerations, and ways to contribute to bird conservation efforts.

Marine Wildlife

Canada, with its vast coastline stretching over 202,080 kilometers, offers an incredible opportunity to encounter diverse marine wildlife. From the pristine waters of the Atlantic Ocean to the rugged beauty of the Pacific coast, Canada is a haven for nature enthusiasts and wildlife lovers alike. In this comprehensive travel guide, we will delve into the captivating world of marine wildlife in Canada, highlighting the best locations to observe these majestic creatures and providing valuable insights to enhance your experience.

The Atlantic Coast:

The Atlantic Coast of Canada is home to a remarkable array of marine wildlife. The rich waters of the Atlantic Ocean provide habitat for various species, including whales, seals, dolphins, and seabirds. Notable destinations along this coast include:
a. Bay of Fundy: Known for having the highest tides in the world, the Bay of Fundy is a prime spot for whale watching. The bay attracts species such as humpback whales, fin whales, minke whales, and the critically endangered North Atlantic right whales.

b. Cape Breton Island: This scenic island offers opportunities for birdwatching, with puffins, bald eagles, and a variety of seabirds inhabiting the cliffs and coastal areas. Visitors can also spot seals, dolphins, and even the occasional whale along the Cabot Trail.

c. Gros Morne National Park: As a UNESCO World Heritage Site, Gros Morne National Park boasts breathtaking fjords and rugged landscapes. Explore the park's coastal areas to spot seabirds, including the rare and endangered Atlantic puffins.

The Gulf of St. Lawrence:
Situated between Newfoundland and Quebec, the Gulf of St. Lawrence is teeming with marine wildlife. Its nutrient-rich waters support an abundance of fish, attracting a diverse range of species. Key locations to explore include:
a. Mingan Archipelago National Park Reserve: This park consists of 30 islands and is renowned for its impressive limestone monoliths. It serves as an important breeding ground for seals and provides habitat for numerous seabird species.

b. Forillon National Park: Located at the tip of the Gaspé Peninsula, Forillon National Park offers opportunities to observe seals, porpoises, and whales. The park's cliffs also provide nesting sites for seabirds, including gannets and common murres.

The Pacific Coast:
Canada's Pacific Coast, encompassing British Columbia and parts of Yukon and Alaska, is a treasure trove of marine wildlife. The nutrient-rich waters of the Pacific Ocean attract a wide range of species, making it an ideal destination for wildlife enthusiasts. Must-visit locations include:
a. Vancouver Island: Home to the Pacific Rim National Park Reserve, Vancouver Island offers fantastic whale watching opportunities. Orcas, humpback whales, gray whales, and several other species can be spotted along the island's coastline.

b. Great Bear Rainforest: Stretching along the central and northern coast of British Columbia, the Great Bear Rainforest is one of the most pristine wilderness areas in the world. Here, visitors may encounter whales, sea lions, sea otters, and various species of seabirds.

Arctic Canada:

The Arctic region of Canada is a unique and remote destination for wildlife enthusiasts seeking an extraordinary experience. While it requires specialized planning and equipment, the rewards are immense. Noteworthy highlights include:

a. Baffin Island: This vast island offers opportunities to spot polar bears, walruses, seals, and Arctic foxes. The icy waters surrounding the island are also home to several whale species, including belugas and bowhead whales.

b. Lancaster Sound: Located in the eastern Arctic, Lancaster Sound is often referred to as the "Serengeti of the North." It serves as a critical summer feeding ground for marine mammals, attracting narwhals, bowhead whales, and seals.

•Winter Sports

Canada, a winter wonderland that offers a plethora of thrilling winter sports activities. From skiing and snowboarding to ice hockey and ice fishing, this vast country provides endless opportunities for adventure and excitement during the colder months. In this Canada travel guide, we will delve into the various winter sports destinations and experiences that you can enjoy across the country. Whether you're an avid sports enthusiast or a casual traveler looking to embrace the beauty of winter, Canada has something for everyone.

I. *Skiing and Snowboarding* :

Canada is renowned for its world-class skiing and snowboarding resorts, attracting enthusiasts from all corners of the globe. The Rocky Mountains in Alberta and British Columbia boast some of the most famous ski destinations, such as Whistler Blackcomb, Banff National Park, and Lake Louise. These resorts offer breathtaking landscapes, diverse terrain, and top-notch facilities catering to all skill levels. Whether you're a beginner or an expert, you can carve your way through powdery slopes and experience the exhilaration of winter sports at their finest.

II. *Ice Hockey* :

No discussion of winter sports in Canada would be complete without mentioning the country's beloved national sport: ice hockey. As you explore various cities, you'll find countless opportunities to watch or even participate in this thrilling sport. Witness the passion and intensity of an NHL game, where some of the world's best players showcase their skills. If you're feeling adventurous, lace up your skates and join a local pick-up game at one of the many outdoor rinks found across the country. Embrace the Canadian spirit and dive headfirst into the heart-pounding action of ice hockey.

III. Ice Skating :

Ice skating is another popular winter activity that can be enjoyed by people of all ages and skill levels. Canada boasts numerous outdoor skating rinks, which transform into magical winter wonderlands during the colder months. The Rideau Canal Skateway in Ottawa, spanning nearly 8 kilometers, is the world's largest naturally frozen ice rink and offers a unique skating experience. Other notable skating locations include Nathan Phillips Square in Toronto, the Forks in Winnipeg, and the frozen ponds in Quebec City. Glide across the glistening ice and immerse yourself in the joyous atmosphere of ice skating in Canada.

IV. Curling :

Curling, a sport that originated in Scotland, has become deeply ingrained in Canadian culture. This team-based sport requires strategy, precision, and teamwork. Try your hand at curling by visiting one of the many curling clubs scattered throughout the country. These clubs often offer beginner-friendly lessons, allowing you to learn the basics of this fascinating sport. Engage in friendly competition and experience the camaraderie that comes with participating in a traditional Canadian pastime.

V. Ice Fishing :

For those seeking a more tranquil winter experience, ice fishing provides a unique opportunity to connect with nature. Canada's countless frozen lakes and rivers offer abundant fishing spots. Grab your fishing gear and venture out onto the ice, drill a hole, and patiently await a nibble. Popular ice fishing destinations include Lake Simcoe in Ontario, Lake Winnipeg in Manitoba, and Lac Saint-Jean in Quebec. Experience the serenity of being surrounded by pristine winter landscapes as you engage in this peaceful yet rewarding winter activity.

Skiing and Snowboarding

Canada, with its vast snowy landscapes and breathtaking mountain ranges, is a paradise for winter sports enthusiasts. Boasting world-class ski resorts, powdery slopes, and stunning alpine scenery, the country offers an unparalleled experience for both skiing and snowboarding enthusiasts. In this comprehensive guide, we will explore the best destinations, top resorts, key considerations, and everything you need to know to embark on an unforgettable skiing and snowboarding adventure in Canada.

Skiing and Snowboarding Destinations:
1.1 Whistler, British Columbia:
Home to North America's largest ski resort with over 8,000 acres of skiable terrain.
Offers a wide range of trails for all skill levels, from gentle slopes to challenging alpine bowls.
Hosted the 2010 Winter Olympics, ensuring world-class facilities and amenities.
Vibrant après-ski scene and a charming pedestrian village with excellent dining and shopping options.

1.2 Banff and Lake Louise, Alberta:

Nestled in the heart of the Canadian Rockies, these resorts offer stunning natural beauty.
Ski at three distinct resorts: Banff Sunshine Village, Lake Louise Ski Resort, and Mount Norquay.

Abundance of light, dry powder snow and varied terrain for skiers and snowboarders of all abilities. Access to Banff National Park, providing a unique opportunity for wildlife sightings and outdoor adventures.

1.3 Mont-Tremblant, Quebec:

Eastern Canada's premier ski destination known for its charming European-style village.
Wide range of trails catering to all levels, from gentle slopes to challenging glades.
Excellent snow conditions and an extensive snowmaking system.
Rich cultural heritage, lively nightlife, and a plethora of off-mountain activities.

Ski Resorts and Facilities:

2.1 World-Class Infrastructure:
Canada's ski resorts offer state-of-the-art lifts, well-groomed slopes, and modern facilities.
Extensive snowmaking systems ensure optimal skiing conditions even during drier periods.
High-quality rental equipment and professional ski schools for beginners or those looking to improve their skills.

2.2 Accommodation Options:

A variety of accommodations are available, ranging from luxury resorts to cozy chalets and budget-friendly lodges.
Many resorts offer ski-in/ski-out accommodations, providing convenience and quick access to the slopes.
Chalets and condos with fully equipped kitchens are ideal for families and groups.

2.3 Après-Ski and Entertainment:

Canada's ski resorts offer a vibrant après-ski scene with cozy pubs, lively bars, and excellent restaurants.
Enjoy live music, cozy fireplaces, and stunning mountain views after a day on the slopes.
Some resorts provide additional recreational activities like ice skating, snowshoeing, and spa facilities.

Skiing vs. Snowboarding:

Both skiing and snowboarding are popular winter sports in Canada, and most resorts cater to both.

Skiers enjoy a more traditional experience with the use of poles for balance and maneuverability. Snowboarding offers a unique thrill, allowing riders to carve through snow using a single board. The choice between skiing and snowboarding ultimately depends on personal preference and skill level.

Climate and Snow Conditions:

Canada's climate varies across its vast expanse, resulting in diverse snow conditions. Western resorts, such as Whistler, benefit from Pacific maritime snow, known for its moisture content and powder quality. Eastern resorts, like Mont-Tremblant, experience colder temperatures and drier snow, providing excellent carving conditions. It's essential to check weather forecasts and snow reports before planning your trip.

Practical Considerations:

5.1 Travel and Transportation:

Canada's major ski destinations are well-connected to international airports, making travel convenient.

Renting a car or utilizing shuttle services are common ways to reach ski resorts from airports or nearby towns.

5.2 Clothing and Gear:

Dressing appropriately for cold temperatures is crucial. Layering is recommended for flexibility and warmth.
Renting or bringing your own ski/snowboarding equipment depends on personal preference and convenience.
Essential gear includes helmets, goggles, gloves, and warm waterproof clothing.

5.3 Safety and Mountain Etiquette:

Familiarize yourself with the mountain's rules and safety guidelines, and always ski or snowboard responsibly.
Carry and use appropriate safety equipment, such as avalanche beacons, when exploring backcountry areas.
Respect other skiers and snowboarders, yield appropriately, and adhere to slope etiquette.

Ice Skating and Hockey

Canada, a land known for its natural beauty, friendly people, and rich cultural heritage, offers a plethora of exciting activities for visitors. Among these, ice skating and hockey hold a special place in the hearts of Canadians. This comprehensive Canada travel guide will delve into the captivating world of ice skating and hockey, highlighting their significance in Canadian culture, exploring iconic venues and events, and providing essential information for visitors seeking to embark on their own icy adventures.

I. Ice Skating in Canada:

A National Pastime:
Ice skating has been an integral part of Canadian culture for centuries. It's not only a beloved winter activity but also a highly competitive sport. Canadians of all ages and skill levels enjoy gliding across frozen lakes, outdoor rinks, and meticulously maintained indoor arenas.

Outdoor Skating Paradises:
Canada boasts numerous enchanting outdoor skating locations. From frozen ponds nestled in

scenic parks to winding ice trails through picturesque landscapes, these natural ice rinks offer a unique and immersive experience. Must-visit destinations include Ottawa's Rideau Canal Skateway, the world's largest skating rink, and the shimmering Lake Louise in Banff National Park.

Indoor Skating Arenas:
For a more controlled and comfortable skating experience, Canada is home to world-class indoor arenas. These modern facilities offer well-maintained ice surfaces, rental equipment, and a range of amenities. Popular venues include the Mattamy Athletic Centre in Toronto, Rogers Place in Edmonton, and the Bell Centre in Montreal, which also host professional hockey games.

Ice Skating Events:
Throughout the winter months, Canada showcases a vibrant array of ice skating events. From festive ice shows to thrilling speed skating competitions, there is something for everyone. Notable events include the Canadian National Skating Championships, the Winterlude Ice Dragon Boat Festival, and the Ice on Whyte Festival in Edmonton.

II. Hockey in Canada:

The Hockey Obsession:
Hockey is the soul of Canadian sports culture. From backyard games to professional leagues, Canadians are passionate about the sport. Hockey unites communities, sparks national pride, and has given birth to some of the greatest players in history.

Exploring Hockey History:
Delve into the rich history of hockey by visiting the Hockey Hall of Fame in Toronto. This renowned museum celebrates the sport's legends, showcases historic memorabilia, and offers interactive exhibits for fans of all ages. It's a must-visit destination for hockey enthusiasts.

Witnessing NHL Action:
To truly experience the intensity of hockey, attending a National Hockey League (NHL) game is a must. Canada boasts several teams, including the Toronto Maple Leafs, Montreal Canadiens, Vancouver Canucks, Calgary Flames, and more. Witness the electrifying atmosphere of a live game and cheer alongside passionate fans.

Playing Hockey:

Immerse yourself in the Canadian hockey culture by participating in a recreational game. Many communities have public ice rinks that offer rental equipment and pickup games for visitors to join. Engaging in this quintessentially Canadian activity provides a unique opportunity to connect with locals and experience the camaraderie firsthand.

III. Practical Information for Visitors:

Weather Considerations:
Ice skating and hockey are predominantly winter activities in Canada, so it's essential to pack appropriate clothing for the cold climate. Layers, warm socks, gloves, and a hat are recommended, along with insulated and waterproof footwear for outdoor skating.

Equipment and Rentals:
Visitors can rent ice skates and hockey equipment from various rental shops near popular ice skating venues and indoor arenas. Alternatively, some hotels and resorts offer rental services as well.

Safety Precautions:
Ice skating and hockey can be physically demanding activities, so it's crucial to prioritize

safety. Always wear a helmet and protective gear when engaging in hockey. For outdoor skating, ensure the ice is thick enough and skate in designated areas to avoid accidents.

Accessibility:
Most indoor arenas and popular outdoor rinks offer accessible facilities, including ramps and elevators. Visitors with mobility challenges can inquire about accessibility options beforehand to ensure a smooth experience.

Winter Festivals

Canada, with its vast snowy landscapes and vibrant cultural heritage, offers a wide array of winter festivals that celebrate the season's magic and bring communities together. From coast to coast, Canadians and visitors alike eagerly anticipate these annual festivities, which showcase the country's diverse traditions, arts, and outdoor activities. In this comprehensive travel guide, we will explore some of the most captivating winter festivals across Canada, highlighting their unique attractions, historical significance, and key details that will help you plan an unforgettable winter getaway.

Winterlude - Ottawa, Ontario and Gatineau, Quebec

Kicking off our journey, Winterlude takes place annually in Ottawa, the capital of Canada, and its neighboring city, Gatineau. Held in February, this iconic festival transforms the cities into a winter wonderland. The Rideau Canal, a UNESCO World Heritage Site, becomes the world's largest ice skating rink, attracting locals and tourists to glide across its frozen surface. Ice sculptors from around the globe gather to showcase their talent, creating breathtaking sculptures. Visitors can also enjoy ice slides, snow playgrounds, cultural performances, and delicious hot beverages as they explore the festival grounds.

Carnaval de Québec - Québec City, Quebec

The Carnaval de Québec, held in Quebec City, is one of the largest winter carnivals in the world, drawing millions of visitors each year. This lively festival, with roots dating back to the 19th century, celebrates Quebecois culture and traditions. The festival features a grand parade, night parades, ice canoe races on the frozen St. Lawrence River, snow sculptures, and exhilarating winter sports like ice skating and snowboarding. Attendees can savor traditional Quebecois cuisine, including piping hot maple taffy, as they immerse themselves in the festival's festive atmosphere.

Festival du Voyageur - Winnipeg, Manitoba
In the heart of the Canadian prairies, the Festival du Voyageur pays homage to the fur trading era and French-Canadian heritage. Taking place in Winnipeg, Manitoba, this 10-day festival showcases lively music, traditional folk dances, historical reenactments, and interactive workshops. Attendees can experience authentic French-Canadian cuisine, including poutine and tourtière, and warm up with a cup of caribou, a traditional winter beverage. The festival also offers snow sculpting competitions, snowshoe races, and horse-drawn sleigh rides, making it a must-visit for those seeking a blend of cultural immersion and outdoor activities.

Winter Carnival - Banff, Alberta
Nestled in the breathtaking Canadian Rockies, the Winter Carnival in Banff, Alberta, is a celebration of winter sports and mountain culture. This festival, held in January, offers a range of activities, from

skiing and snowboarding in the world-class slopes of Banff National Park to ice climbing, dogsledding, and ice fishing. Visitors can marvel at ice sculptures, take part in snowshoe races, or enjoy live music performances in cozy mountain lodges. The Winter Carnival perfectly captures the essence of Canada's winter wilderness and is a must-visit for outdoor enthusiasts and nature lovers.

Quebec Winter Festival - Gatineau, Quebec

Situated just across the river from Ottawa, the Quebec Winter Festival is one of the largest winter events in North America. Held in Gatineau Park, this festival offers a range of activities, including snowshoeing, cross-country skiing, and ice fishing. Visitors can witness the exhilarating ice canoe race on the frozen Ottawa River or try their hand at ice sculpture carving. The festival also features live music, dance performances, and traditional cuisine, highlighting the region's unique Franco-Canadian culture. With its spectacular outdoor setting and diverse program, the Quebec Winter Festival promises an unforgettable winter experience.

Winter festivals in Canada are much more than mere celebrations; they embody the spirit of the country's winter wonderland and its rich cultural heritage. From the majestic Rockies in Banff to the historic streets of Quebec City, each festival offers a unique blend of outdoor activities, artistic displays, and traditional cuisine that captivates visitors of all ages and interests. Whether you're an avid winter sports enthusiast, a lover of arts and culture, or simply seeking a memorable winter escape, Canada's winter festivals provide a captivating experience that will leave you with lifelong memories. So, pack your warmest clothes and embark on an adventure to discover the beauty and magic of winter in Canada.

Chapter seven

Unique Canadian Experiences

•*Polar Bear Tours*

When it comes to wildlife encounters, few experiences can match the awe-inspiring sight of polar bears in their natural habitat. Canada, specifically the northern regions of Manitoba and Nunavut, offers some of the best opportunities to witness these magnificent creatures up close. In this Canada travel guide , we will explore the thrilling world of polar bear tours and the enchanting landscapes they encompass.

Location:
The polar bear tours in Canada primarily focus on Churchill, a small town situated on the western shore of Hudson Bay in Manitoba. Known as the "Polar Bear Capital of the World," Churchill serves

as the gateway to the bears' migration route and is an ideal base for embarking on Arctic adventures.

Tour Seasons:
The best time to witness polar bears in Churchill is during the fall, from October to November. This period coincides with the bears' annual migration to the sea ice, where they hunt for seals. During this time, several tour operators offer guided expeditions that ensure unforgettable encounters with these remarkable creatures.

Tour Options:
Various tour options are available to suit different preferences and budgets. From one-day excursions to multi-day expeditions, travelers can choose the experience that suits them best. It is essential to book in advance, as these tours are popular and tend to fill up quickly.

Tundra Buggy Tours:
One of the most popular ways to explore the Arctic landscape and observe polar bears is by embarking on a tundra buggy tour. These specially designed vehicles, reminiscent of oversized buses, are built to navigate the rugged terrain and offer excellent visibility for wildlife viewing. Equipped with large

windows and raised platforms, they provide optimal vantage points for spotting bears in their natural habitat.

Dog Sledding and Snowshoeing:
For those seeking a more immersive Arctic experience, dog sledding and snowshoeing tours are available. These activities allow travelers to traverse the snowy landscapes and gain a deeper understanding of the region's natural beauty. While encountering polar bears is less common on these tours, the chance to explore the pristine wilderness and enjoy the company of friendly huskies is an adventure in itself.

Tundra Lodge:
For an even more immersive experience, some tour operators offer stays at the Tundra Lodge, a unique accommodation situated directly on the tundra. This mobile lodge provides visitors with the opportunity to observe polar bears from the comfort of a warm, cozy environment. Imagine waking up to the sight of a polar bear just outside your window or witnessing the northern lights dancing across the sky while nestled in this remote Arctic sanctuary.

Safety and Conservation:

It is important to note that polar bear tours prioritize the safety of both travelers and wildlife. Local guides and experienced naturalists accompany visitors, providing informative commentary and ensuring responsible behavior. As polar bears are wild animals, it is crucial to respect their space and observe them from a safe distance.

Polar bear tours in Canada offer a rare chance to witness these incredible creatures in their natural habitat, creating memories that will last a lifetime. Whether you choose a tundra buggy tour, a dog sledding adventure, or a stay at the Tundra Lodge, the beauty of the Arctic landscape and the majesty of the polar bears will leave you in awe. So, pack your winter gear, embrace the spirit of adventure, and embark on an unforgettable journey to the captivating world of polar bears in Canada.

•Aurora Borealis Viewing

Canada, with its vast wilderness and northern latitude, offers one of the most mesmerizing natural wonders on Earth—the Aurora Borealis. Known as the Northern Lights, this celestial spectacle has enchanted travelers and photographers for centuries. In this comprehensive Canada travel guide, we will explore the best locations, optimal viewing times, and essential tips to enhance your Aurora Borealis experience.

What are the Aurora Borealis?

The Aurora Borealis is a captivating light display that occurs when charged particles from the sun collide with Earth's atmosphere. This collision releases energy in the form of colorful lights, predominantly green but often accompanied by hues of pink, purple, and blue. Canada's high latitudes and minimal light pollution make it an ideal destination for witnessing this breathtaking phenomenon.

Best Locations for Aurora Borealis Viewing in Canada

a) Yellowknife, Northwest Territories: Renowned as the Aurora Capital of North America, Yellowknife offers a combination of clear skies, favorable weather conditions, and easy accessibility. Visitors can explore the nearby Wood Buffalo National Park or opt for organized tours to chase the lights.

b) Whitehorse, Yukon: Nestled amidst the rugged landscapes of Yukon, Whitehorse is another prime location for Aurora Borealis viewing. The nearby Yukon Wildlife Preserve and Takhini Hot Springs add to the overall experience.

c) Churchill, Manitoba: This remote town on Hudson Bay provides a unique opportunity to witness the Northern Lights against the backdrop of frozen tundra and the possibility of encountering polar bears.

d) Banff and Jasper National Parks, Alberta: While known for their stunning mountain scenery, these national parks occasionally treat visitors to the Aurora Borealis. Combining nature and the lights offers a memorable experience.

Optimal Viewing Times and Weather Conditions
The Aurora Borealis is visible in Canada's northern regions throughout the year, but the optimal viewing season is from late August to early April. During this period, the nights are long, and the chances of clear skies are higher. Avoiding the full moon period and choosing nights with little to no

light pollution will enhance your viewing experience.

Checking the local weather forecasts and aurora activity predictions is crucial. Websites and apps like Space Weather Live and AuroraMax provide real-time data on solar activity and the likelihood of auroral displays. Patience is key, as the lights can be elusive and may require multiple nights of observation.

Tips for an Enriching Aurora Borealis Experience

a) Dress appropriately: The Canadian North can be extremely cold, even in milder months. Layering your clothing, including thermal wear, insulating jackets, hats, gloves, and warm boots, is essential to stay comfortable during long hours of outdoor viewing.

b) Capture the moment: Bring a tripod and a camera capable of long exposures to capture stunning photographs of the Northern Lights. Experiment with different settings and manual modes to achieve the best results.

c) Consider guided tours: Joining an organized Aurora Borealis tour allows for expert guidance, local knowledge, and increased chances of finding the lights. Experienced guides know the best spots and can offer insights into the cultural and natural history of the region.

d) Embrace the local culture: Immerse yourself in the local Indigenous culture, as many communities in Canada's northern regions have a deep spiritual connection with the Northern Lights. Attend cultural events, listen to stories, and learn about the significance of the lights in Indigenous folklore.

Other Attractions and Activities in Canada's North

Canada's northern regions offer more than just the Aurora Borealis. Visitors can indulge in a range of activities, such as dog sledding, snowmobiling, ice fishing, and exploring ice caves. Wildlife enthusiasts can spot majestic creatures like moose, caribou, and Arctic foxes. Additionally, experiencing the midnight sun during the summer months adds to the uniqueness of the region.

Witnessing the ethereal dance of the Aurora Borealis is an unforgettable experience that Canada's northern regions offer. From Yellowknife's accessible beauty to Churchill's remote charm, each location provides a distinct opportunity to admire this natural phenomenon. By following the tips outlined in this Canada travel guide, you'll be well-prepared to maximize your chances of encountering the mesmerizing Northern Lights and create lasting memories of this extraordinary journey.

•Dog Sledding

One such adventure that embodies the spirit of Canada's rugged wilderness is dog sledding. Immersed in the beauty of the Great White North, dog sledding offers a unique way to explore the snowy landscapes while forging an unbreakable bond with these remarkable canine athletes. In this Canada travel guide, we will delve into the fascinating world of dog sledding, its history, popular destinations, best times to visit, and practical tips to help you plan an unforgettable dog sledding experience in Canada.

I. The History and Culture of Dog Sledding

Origins of dog sledding: Dog sledding has deep roots in Indigenous cultures, where sled dogs played a crucial role in transportation and survival. The significance of sled dogs: The symbiotic relationship between mushers (dog sled drivers) and their dogs, and the vital role sled dogs played in the exploration of the Canadian Arctic.

The modern evolution of dog sledding: From a means of transportation to a recreational activity, dog sledding has transformed into a thrilling adventure sport.

II. Top Dog Sledding Destinations in Canada
A. Yukon

Whitehorse: The capital city with various dog sledding tours, including multi-day expeditions through the breathtaking Yukon wilderness.
Dawson City: Experience the exhilaration of racing sled dogs and learn about the history of the Klondike Gold Rush.
Teslin: Explore the stunning landscapes of Teslin Lake and participate in dog sledding adventures tailored to different experience levels.

B. Canadian Rockies

Canmore, Alberta: Embark on dog sledding adventures in the majestic Rocky Mountains, surrounded by picturesque vistas.
Banff National Park: Discover the beauty of the Canadian Rockies while experiencing dog sledding through snowy forests and ice-covered lakes.
C. Quebec

Mont-Tremblant: Enjoy a quintessential Canadian winter experience with dog sledding excursions through Quebec's picturesque Laurentian Mountains.
Charlevoix: Experience the magic of winter landscapes along the Saint-Lawrence River during dog sledding tours in this charming region.

III. Best Times to Go Dog Sledding in Canada

Winter season: From December to March, Canada offers ideal conditions for dog sledding, with ample snow cover and milder temperatures in many regions.

Consider regional variations: Weather conditions can vary across Canada, so it's essential to research specific destinations to determine the best time to go dog sledding in each region.

IV. Practical Tips for Dog Sledding in Canada

Choosing a reputable tour operator: Research and select a tour operator that prioritizes the welfare of their dogs and provides a safe and authentic experience.
Physical fitness and preparation: Dog sledding requires physical exertion, so ensure you are in reasonably good health and adequately prepared for the activity.
Dressing for the cold: Layering clothing and wearing appropriate gear, such as thermal jackets, pants, gloves, and boots, is essential for staying warm in the sub-zero temperatures.
Interacting with the dogs: Learn about dog sledding etiquette and how to interact with the dogs respectfully, understanding their needs and commands.

Dog sledding in Canada is a unique and thrilling adventure that allows you to immerse yourself in the vast, pristine wilderness of the Great White North. The cultural and historical significance of dog sledding, combined with the breathtaking landscapes, makes it a must-do experience.

•Canoeing and Kayaking

Canada, with its vast and diverse landscape, offers an unparalleled playground for outdoor enthusiasts. From majestic mountains to pristine lakes and winding rivers, this country is a paradise for canoeing and kayaking enthusiasts. In this Canada travel guide, we will explore the best destinations, tips, and experiences for those seeking unforgettable adventures on the water.

Canada's Top Canoeing and Kayaking Destinations:

1.1 Algonquin Provincial Park, Ontario: Renowned for its picturesque lakes, dense forests, and abundant wildlife, Algonquin Provincial Park is a prime destination for canoeing and kayaking in Canada. With over 2,400 lakes and 1,200 kilometers of rivers, this park offers a range of paddling experiences suitable for all skill levels.

1.2 Bowron Lakes Provincial Park, British Columbia:
Located in the heart of the Cariboo Mountains, Bowron Lakes Provincial Park is a canoeist's paradise. The park's highlight is the Bowron Lakes Circuit, a 116-kilometer route that encompasses several lakes, rivers, and portages. This multi-day adventure promises breathtaking scenery and opportunities to spot wildlife like moose, bears, and eagles.

1.3 Nahanni National Park Reserve, Northwest Territories:
Recognized as a UNESCO World Heritage Site, Nahanni National Park Reserve boasts the iconic South Nahanni River, which carves its way through rugged canyons and vast wilderness. Paddling through the park provides a thrilling journey for experienced kayakers, with opportunities to witness majestic waterfalls and immerse in the untouched beauty of the Canadian North.

1.4 Gulf Islands, British Columbia:
For those seeking a more relaxed and coastal paddling experience, the Gulf Islands archipelago is a fantastic choice. Situated between Vancouver Island and the mainland, this region offers calm

waters, stunning shorelines, and an abundance of marine life. Kayakers can explore numerous islands, visit quaint coastal communities, and revel in the breathtaking beauty of the Pacific Northwest.

Essential Tips for Canoeing and Kayaking in Canada:

2.1 Safety Precautions:
Before embarking on any paddling adventure, it is essential to prioritize safety. This includes wearing personal flotation devices (PFDs), informing others about your plans, checking weather conditions, and carrying necessary safety equipment, such as a whistle, a map, and a first aid kit.

2.2 Equipment and Gear:
When planning a canoeing or kayaking trip in Canada, ensure you have the appropriate equipment and gear. This includes selecting the right vessel, paddles, waterproof storage containers, camping gear, and clothing suitable for the prevailing weather conditions. Renting equipment is also an option in many popular destinations.

2.3 Skill and Experience:
Consider your skill level and experience when choosing a paddling destination in Canada. Some

areas, like remote rivers in the North, require advanced skills and wilderness experience. Beginners can opt for more accessible locations with calm waters and easy navigation. Joining guided trips or taking lessons from local outfitters is a great way to enhance your skills and confidence.

2.4 Leave No Trace Principles:
Respecting and preserving the natural environment should be a priority for all paddlers. Adhere to the Leave No Trace principles, which include packing out all trash, minimizing campfire impacts, respecting wildlife, and staying on designated trails or campsites. This ensures that future generations can enjoy the beauty of Canada's waterways.

Experiences and Unique Adventures:
3.1 Wildlife Encounters:
Canada's waterways offer incredible opportunities to encounter a diverse array of wildlife. Keep an eye out for moose, beavers, loons, eagles, and other fascinating creatures that call these habitats home. Remember to maintain a safe distance and observe without disturbing their natural behavior.
3.2 Indigenous Cultural Experiences:
Many regions in Canada have a rich indigenous heritage, and paddling presents an excellent

opportunity to learn about and appreciate these cultures. Explore the traditional territories of indigenous communities, participate in cultural events, and engage with local guides to gain insights into their history, traditions, and connection to the land.

3.3 Fishing:
Canada is renowned for its exceptional fishing opportunities. Pack your fishing gear and try your luck catching various species, such as trout, salmon, and pike. Familiarize yourself with fishing regulations and obtain the necessary permits to ensure responsible angling practices.

Embarking on a canoeing or kayaking adventure in Canada is an experience like no other. With its stunning landscapes, diverse waterways, and opportunities for wildlife encounters, Canada offers an unrivaled playground for outdoor enthusiasts. By following safety guidelines, respecting the environment, and immersing oneself in the local culture, travelers can create unforgettable memories while exploring the country's remarkable waterways. So, pack your gear, embrace the spirit of adventure, and embark on a journey to discover the beauty of Canada from a paddler's perspective.

Chapter Eight

Practical Information

•Health and Safety

Canada is known for its vibrant cities, and welcoming people. As you plan your trip to Canada, it is crucial to prioritize your health and safety. This guide aims to provide you with essential information on healthcare services, common health risks, safety measures, and emergency contacts to ensure a smooth and secure travel experience across the vast expanse of Canada.

Healthcare System in Canada:

Canada boasts a universal healthcare system that provides basic medical services to all residents and citizens. The healthcare system is funded by the government, ensuring that necessary medical care is accessible to everyone. It is advisable, however, for visitors to obtain travel health insurance to cover potential medical costs not covered by the provincial healthcare system.

Travel Health Insurance:
Visitors to Canada should acquire travel health insurance to safeguard themselves against any unforeseen medical expenses. This insurance typically covers emergency medical treatments, hospital stays, prescription medications, and medical evacuation if necessary. It is essential to review the coverage details and ensure that it meets your specific needs.

Pre-Travel Health Planning:
Before embarking on your journey, it is recommended to consult your healthcare provider or a travel medicine specialist. They can provide guidance on necessary vaccinations, medications, and preventive measures based on your health status and the regions you plan to visit in Canada. Routine vaccinations, such as measles, mumps, rubella (MMR), diphtheria-tetanus-pertussis (DTaP), and influenza, should be up to date.

Common Health Risks in Canada:
a) Extreme Weather: Canada experiences a wide range of climates, from freezing temperatures in the

north to scorching summers in the south. It is crucial to dress appropriately and be prepared for extreme weather conditions to prevent frostbite, hypothermia, or heat-related illnesses.

b) Tick-Borne Diseases: Lyme disease, transmitted through ticks, is prevalent in certain regions of Canada. Wearing protective clothing, using insect repellents, and conducting regular tick checks can reduce the risk of contracting tick-borne illnesses.

c) Food and Water Safety: Overall, food and water safety standards in Canada are high. However, it is advisable to practice general food hygiene precautions, such as washing hands before meals and consuming bottled or treated water in remote areas.

Safety Measures:

a) Personal Safety: Canada is generally considered a safe country to visit, but it is always important to remain vigilant, especially in crowded tourist areas or urban centers. Be cautious of your belongings, avoid isolated areas at night, and familiarize yourself with local emergency services.

b) Transportation Safety: If you plan to drive in Canada, ensure that you have a valid driver's license and familiarize yourself with local traffic rules and regulations. Use seat belts at all times, and refrain from driving under the influence of alcohol or drugs.

c) Outdoor Safety: Canada's natural beauty attracts adventure seekers, but it is essential to prioritize safety during outdoor activities. Research and follow safety guidelines for activities like hiking, camping, and wildlife encounters. Inform someone about your plans, carry essential supplies, and be mindful of weather conditions and wildlife behavior.

Emergency Contacts:
In case of emergencies, it is crucial to know the relevant emergency contacts in Canada:

Emergency Services (Police, Fire, Ambulance): **911**
Local Police Non-Emergency: Look up the local non-emergency number for the area you are visiting.
Health Link (Non-Emergency Health Advice): Dial **811** in most provinces.

Prioritizing your health and safety while traveling in Canada is essential to ensure a memorable and incident-free journey. By understanding the healthcare system, obtaining travel health insurance, and being aware of common health risks and safety measures, you can enjoy Canada's diverse landscapes and vibrant culture with peace of mind. Remember to plan ahead, consult healthcare professionals, and adhere to local regulations for a safe and enjoyable experience in the Great White North.

Communication and Internet Access

Canada, the second-largest country in the world by land area, offers breathtaking landscapes, diverse cultures, and vibrant cities. As a traveler exploring this vast nation, it is essential to understand the communication options and internet access available to stay connected with loved ones, access essential information, and make the most of your trip. In this guide, we will provide an overview of the communication infrastructure in Canada, including mobile networks, internet connectivity, and popular messaging services. We will also highlight practical tips and resources to ensure seamless communication throughout your Canadian adventure.

Mobile Networks in Canada :

Canada boasts a reliable and extensive mobile network infrastructure that covers most urban areas and major highways. The country's three major mobile network operators—Bell, Rogers, and Telus—provide nationwide coverage with various plans to suit different needs and budgets. These networks operate on advanced technologies such as 4G LTE and are gradually rolling out 5G capabilities.

When traveling to Canada, it is important to check if your existing mobile service provider offers international roaming options. Roaming charges can be significant, so consider purchasing a local SIM card upon arrival to benefit from more affordable rates. Local SIM cards are readily available at airports, convenience stores, and mobile network provider outlets. Ensure that your device is unlocked and compatible with Canadian networks before purchasing a local SIM card.

Internet Access in Canada :

Internet connectivity is widespread in Canada, particularly in urban areas and popular tourist destinations. Most hotels, hostels, cafes, and public spaces offer free or paid Wi-Fi access for guests. Major cities, including Toronto, Vancouver, and Montreal, provide extensive coverage of public Wi-Fi networks, making it convenient to stay connected while exploring these urban hubs. In addition to Wi-Fi access, travelers can also rely on mobile data plans for internet connectivity. Major mobile network operators offer data packages suitable for tourists, enabling seamless browsing, navigation, and social media usage throughout your trip. Keep in mind that data plans can vary in terms of data limits and prices, so compare available options before making a decision.

Messaging and Communication Apps :
Staying in touch with friends and family or connecting with fellow travelers is made easier through messaging and communication apps. While traditional SMS and phone calls remain viable options, these apps provide a cost-effective alternative, especially for international travelers. WhatsApp, one of the most popular messaging apps worldwide, is widely used in Canada. It allows users to send text messages, make voice and video calls, and share multimedia content over Wi-Fi or mobile

data. Other popular messaging apps include Facebook Messenger, iMessage (exclusive to Apple devices), and Telegram.

Practical Tips for Staying Connected :
a. Purchase a Travel SIM Card: If you plan to extensively use your mobile phone during your stay in Canada, consider purchasing a travel SIM card. These cards are available at various price points and provide specific allowances for calls, texts, and data.
b. Plan for Roaming Charges: If you prefer to use your existing mobile service provider, check their international roaming rates and policies before arriving in Canada. Be mindful of potential charges for calls, texts, and data usage, as they can quickly accumulate.

c. Download Offline Maps: To navigate Canadian cities and regions without relying on constant internet access, download offline maps before your trip. Apps like Google Maps and Maps.me offer offline functionality, allowing you to access maps, directions, and points of interest without an active internet connection.

d. Utilize Public Wi-Fi Networks Securely: While public Wi-Fi networks are convenient, exercise caution when accessing sensitive information, such as online banking or personal accounts. To ensure your data remains secure, consider using a virtual private network (VPN) when connecting to public Wi-Fi.

e. Check Local Coverage: Before embarking on remote adventures in Canada's vast wilderness, research the local coverage of mobile networks. Some rural areas may have limited or no mobile network coverage, so plan accordingly and inform others of your itinerary.

In this digital age, staying connected while traveling is crucial, and Canada provides a robust communication infrastructure to support travelers. With reliable mobile networks, extensive internet connectivity, and popular messaging apps, you can easily communicate with loved ones, access information, and share your Canadian experiences.

Whether you choose to rely on your existing mobile service provider's international roaming options or purchase a local SIM card, staying connected in

Canada is convenient and accessible. Additionally, public Wi-Fi networks and offline maps offer further flexibility for communication and navigation throughout the country.

As with any international travel, it is important to plan ahead, research the available options, and ensure that you have the necessary tools to stay connected. By following the practical tips provided in this guide, you can enjoy seamless communication and internet access throughout your Canadian adventure.

Embrace the beauty of Canada's landscapes, immerse yourself in its vibrant cultures, and share your experiences with the world—all while staying connected in the Great White North.

Local Customs and Etiquette

Canada is known for its friendly people, and diverse cultural heritage. As you embark on your journey to explore this vast nation, it is essential to familiarize yourself with the local customs and etiquette to ensure a pleasant and respectful experience. This travel guide will provide you with valuable insights into the cultural norms, social expectations, and customary practices in Canada.

Greetings and Politeness:
Canadians are generally polite and friendly, and a warm greeting is customary when meeting someone new. A firm handshake and direct eye contact are standard during introductions. It is also common to address people using their first names, even in formal settings. Please note that Quebec, a predominantly French-speaking province, tends to observe a more formal approach, with a preference for titles and surnames.

Apologies and "Sorry" Culture:
Canadians are famous for their use of the word "sorry." It is not uncommon for Canadians to apologize for minor inconveniences or accidental encounters. This practice reflects their politeness and consideration for others. If you accidentally bump into someone or make a mistake, a sincere apology will be appreciated.

Punctuality and Time Management:

Being punctual is highly valued in Canadian culture. Arriving a few minutes early or on time for social and business engagements is considered respectful. If you anticipate being late, it is polite to inform the other party in advance. Time management is crucial in Canada, so it is essential to respect scheduled appointments and meetings.

Personal Space and Queuing:

Canadians value personal space and tend to stand at arm's length from each other during conversations. It is important to respect this distance and avoid invading someone's personal space. When queuing in public places, such as lines at the grocery store or public transportation, wait your turn patiently and avoid jumping ahead.

Multiculturalism and Diversity:

Canada prides itself on being a multicultural society that celebrates diversity. Canadians are generally open-minded and accepting of different cultures, religions, and lifestyles. Respecting and appreciating the diversity you encounter during your travels will help foster positive interactions with locals.

Dining Etiquette:

When dining with Canadians, it is customary to wait until everyone is seated before starting the meal. Table manners are relatively informal, but it is polite to chew with your mouth closed, avoid talking with food in your mouth, and use utensils appropriately. Tipping is customary in restaurants, and it is generally expected to leave a gratuity of 15-20% of the bill, unless a service charge is already included.

Social Etiquette:

During social gatherings, Canadians appreciate polite and respectful conversations. It is customary to engage in small talk and show genuine interest in others. Avoid discussing sensitive topics such as politics, religion, and personal finances unless the other party initiates such discussions. Canada's official languages are English and French, so it is helpful to be aware of language preferences based on the region you are visiting.

Dress Code:

Canada's dress code varies depending on the occasion, location, and climate. In general, Canadians dress casually for most day-to-day activities. However, certain formal events, such as weddings or business meetings, may require more formal attire. It is advisable to check the dress code guidelines beforehand to ensure appropriate dressing.

Outdoor Etiquette:
Canada's vast natural landscapes offer numerous opportunities for outdoor activities. When hiking, camping, or exploring national parks, it is essential to follow Leave No Trace principles, which emphasize leaving nature undisturbed and taking any waste with you. Respecting wildlife and adhering to park rules and regulations are crucial to maintaining the beauty and sustainability of these natural spaces.

Cultural Sensitivity:
As a visitor, being culturally sensitive is vital. Understanding and respecting Indigenous culture and history is especially important in Canada. Treat Indigenous communities, traditions, and sacred sites with the utmost respect, and seek permission before entering or photographing these areas. Learn about the local customs and practices of the region you are visiting to show your appreciation and avoid unintentionally causing offense.

Exploring Canada is an exciting adventure, and understanding the customs and etiquette of the country will enhance your experience. Canadians are known for their warm hospitality and politeness, and respecting their cultural norms will help foster positive interactions and create lasting memories. By embracing the diversity, natural beauty, and rich cultural heritage of Canada, you will undoubtedly have a remarkable journey through this magnificent country.

Emergency Services

When embarking on a journey to Canada, it is crucial to be aware of the country's emergency services to ensure a safe and secure travel experience. Canada boasts a well-established network of emergency services that are readily available to assist residents and visitors in times of crisis. From medical emergencies to natural disasters, Canadian emergency services are equipped with the necessary resources, technology, and highly trained personnel to handle a wide range of situations. This comprehensive guide will provide an overview of the emergency services in Canada, including healthcare, police, and fire services, offering valuable insights for travelers to plan their trips with confidence.

Healthcare Services:

Canada's healthcare system is known for its universal coverage, ensuring that every resident and visitor has access to essential medical care. The country's emergency medical services (EMS) are designed to provide rapid response and transportation to medical facilities. The EMS is accessible nationwide, and the emergency telephone number to dial is 911. Upon dialing, highly trained emergency medical dispatchers will assess the situation and dispatch the appropriate emergency medical personnel to the scene. Paramedics and ambulance services are available 24/7, equipped with advanced medical equipment to handle emergencies and transport patients to the nearest hospital or medical facility. In larger cities, specialized medical teams, such as trauma response units and air ambulance services, are also available to handle critical situations.

Police Services:

The Royal Canadian Mounted Police (RCMP) is the federal and national law enforcement agency in Canada. It is responsible for maintaining peace, enforcing laws, and ensuring public safety in areas without provincial or municipal police forces. In addition to the RCMP, Canada has provincial and municipal police services that operate at the regional and local levels. These services are responsible for maintaining law and order within their respective jurisdictions. Travelers can expect a visible police presence across the country, ensuring a sense of security. In case of emergencies or to report a crime, dialing 911 will connect you to the appropriate police service. The police services in Canada are highly trained and equipped to respond promptly to emergencies, offer assistance, and investigate incidents.

Fire Services:

Canada's fire services play a crucial role in responding to fires, hazardous incidents, and other emergencies. Each province and territory has its own fire services, which include municipal fire departments and volunteer fire brigades. The fire services in Canada follow stringent protocols and undergo rigorous training to ensure effective response and prevention of fire-related emergencies. In case of a fire or any other emergency that requires the assistance of the fire services, dial 911, and the call will be directed to the appropriate local fire department. Firefighters are trained not only in firefighting but also in various rescue techniques, such as water rescues, high-angle rescues, and hazardous materials response.

Natural Disaster Preparedness:
Canada is prone to various natural disasters, including wildfires, floods, earthquakes, and severe weather events. As a responsible traveler, it is essential to be aware of the potential risks and the emergency services available to respond to these situations. The Government of Canada has comprehensive disaster management plans in place to mitigate the impact of natural disasters and protect residents and visitors. These plans involve collaboration between various emergency services, government agencies, and communities to provide timely warnings, evacuation procedures, and emergency support. Travelers are encouraged to monitor weather conditions, follow local advisories, and heed evacuation orders when necessary.

Additional Emergency Services:

In addition to healthcare, police, and fire services, Canada offers several other emergency services that contribute to the safety and well-being of travelers. These include search and rescue services, coast guard services, and border services. Search and rescue teams are highly skilled and well-equipped to respond to incidents in remote areas, such as national parks, hiking trails, and backcountry skiing areas. The Canadian Coast Guard operates in coastal regions and navigable waterways, providing marine search and rescue services, icebreaking, and maritime security. Border services ensure the safety and security of Canada's borders, including airport security and customs.

Canada prioritizes the safety and security of its residents and visitors through a well-established network of emergency services. Travelers can have peace of mind knowing that in case of an emergency, the country's healthcare, police, and fire services, along with other specialized services, are available 24/7 to provide prompt assistance. Understanding the emergency services in Canada, including how to contact them and their capabilities, is crucial for any traveler planning a trip to this beautiful country. By being aware and prepared, travelers can enjoy their visit to Canada with confidence, knowing that help is just a phone call away.

Useful Phrases and Vocabulary

Canada is a vast and diverse country, known for its stunning landscapes, friendly people, and rich cultural heritage. Whether you're planning a trip to explore the bustling cities, marvel at the majestic mountains, or immerse yourself in the vibrant culture, knowing some essential phrases and vocabulary will greatly enhance your travel experience. This Canada travel guide aims to provide you with a comprehensive list of useful phrases and vocabulary to help you navigate your way through this beautiful country.

Greetings and Basic Phrases:
Hello: "Bonjour" (in French, predominantly spoken in Quebec) or "Hello" (in English, commonly spoken throughout Canada).

Goodbye: "Au revoir" (French) or "Goodbye" (English).

Thank you: "Merci" (French) or "Thank you" (English).

Please: "S'il vous plaît" (French) or "Please" (English).

Excuse me: "Excusez-moi" (French) or "Excuse me" (English).

Yes: "Oui" (French) or "Yes" (English).

No: "Non" (French) or "No" (English).

Sorry: Canadians are known for their politeness, so you might hear "Sorry" quite often. It is used to express apologies or to get someone's attention.

Directions and Transportation:

Where is...? - "Où est...?" (French) or "Where is...?" (English).

Bus station: "Gare d'autobus" (French) or "Bus station" (English).

Train station: "Gare de train" (French) or "Train station" (English).

Airport: "Aéroport" (French) or "Airport" (English).

Can you help me? - "Pouvez-vous m'aider?" (French) or "Can you help me?" (English).

How much does it cost? - "Combien ça coûte?" (French) or "How much does it cost?" (English).

Left: "Gauche" (French) or "Left" (English).

Right: "Droite" (French) or "Right" (English).

Straight ahead: "Tout droit" (French) or "Straight ahead" (English).

Where can I find a taxi? - "Où puis-je trouver un taxi?" (French) or "Where can I find a taxi?" (English).

Accommodation:

Hotel: "Hôtel" (French) or "Hotel" (English).

Room: "Chambre" (French) or "Room" (English).

Reservation: "Réservation" (French) or "Reservation" (English).

Check-in: "Enregistrement" (French) or "Check-in" (English).

Check-out: "Départ" (French) or "Check-out" (English).

Key: "Clé" (French) or "Key" (English).

Do you have any vacancies? - "Avez-vous des chambres de libre?" (French) or "Do you have any vacancies?" (English).

Can I see the room? - "Puis-je voir la chambre?" (French) or "Can I see the room?" (English).

Food and Dining:

Menu: "Menu" (French) or "Menu" (English).

Breakfast: "Déjeuner" (French) or "Breakfast" (English).

Lunch: "Dîner" (French) or "Lunch" (English).

Dinner: "Souper" (French, mainly in Quebec) or "Dinner" (English).

I would like... - "Je voudrais..." (French) or "I would like..." (English).

What do you recommend? - "Que recommandez-vous?" (French) or "What do you recommend?" (English).

The bill, please: "L'addition, s'il vous plaît" (French) or "The bill, please" (English).

Can I have the check? - "Puis-je avoir l'addition?" (French) or "Can I have the check?" (English).

Shopping:

Store: "Magasin" (French) or "Store" (English).

How much does it cost? - "Combien ça coûte?" (French) or "How much does it cost?" (English).

Can I try it on? - "Puis-je l'essayer?" (French) or "Can I try it on?" (English).

Do you accept credit cards? - "Acceptez-vous les cartes de crédit?" (French) or "Do you accept credit cards?" (English).

Do you have this in a different color/size? - "Avez-vous cela dans une autre couleur/taille?" (French) or "Do you have this in a different color/size?" (English).

Emergencies:

Help: "Au secours" (French) or "Help" (English).

Police: "Police" (French) or "Police" (English).

Hospital: "Hôpital" (French) or "Hospital" (English).

I need a doctor: "J'ai besoin d'un médecin" (French) or "I need a doctor" (English).
Where is the nearest pharmacy? - "Où est la pharmacie la plus proche?" (French) or "Where is the nearest pharmacy?" (English).
Call an ambulance: "Appelez une ambulance" (French) or "Call an ambulance" (English).

Mastering some essential phrases and vocabulary before your trip to Canada will greatly enhance your travel experience and make your interactions with locals more enjoyable. While English is widely spoken across the country, particularly in urban areas, learning a few basic French phrases can be helpful in Quebec and other francophone regions. Remember, Canadians are known for their friendliness and helpfulness, so don't hesitate to ask for assistance if needed. Immerse yourself in the beauty of Canada's diverse landscapes, indulge in its rich culture, and have an unforgettable journey across this magnificent country.

Chapter Nine

Traveling with Children

•*Family-Friendly Destinations*

Canada, known for its stunning landscapes, vibrant cities, and diverse cultural experiences, offers an array of family-friendly destinations that cater to travelers of all ages. From breathtaking national parks to educational museums and thrilling outdoor adventures, Canada has something to offer every member of the family. In this comprehensive travel guide, we will explore the top family-friendly destinations across the country, ensuring an unforgettable and enriching experience for everyone.

Vancouver, British Columbia:

Located on the west coast, Vancouver provides an ideal mix of urban attractions and natural beauty. Families can explore the iconic Stanley Park, a 1,000-acre urban oasis with scenic trails, a mini-train, and the Vancouver Aquarium. Science World offers interactive exhibits and an OMNIMAX theater, while the Capilano Suspension Bridge Park provides an adrenaline-filled experience amidst the treetops. The nearby Granville Island offers a lively public market and a variety of artisan shops, perfect for family exploration.

Toronto, Ontario:

As Canada's largest city, Toronto offers a plethora of family-friendly attractions. The Royal Ontario Museum boasts fascinating exhibits on dinosaurs, ancient Egypt, and biodiversity. The Ontario Science Centre is an interactive learning hub with hands-on exhibits and a planetarium. Take a trip to the top of the iconic CN Tower for stunning panoramic views of the city. Toronto Islands, located just a short ferry ride away, provide beautiful beaches, bike rentals, and picnic spots, making it an ideal day trip for families.

Quebec City, Quebec:

With its charming European ambiance and rich history, Quebec City is an excellent family-friendly destination. Explore the historic streets of Old Quebec, a UNESCO World Heritage site, and visit the iconic Chateau Frontenac. The Musee de la Civilisation offers engaging exhibits and interactive activities for children. Families can also enjoy a leisurely stroll along the Plains of Abraham, a historic park with beautiful views of the St. Lawrence River. Don't forget to try maple taffy, a sweet treat made by pouring hot maple syrup onto the snow.

Banff National Park, Alberta:

Nestled in the Canadian Rockies, Banff National Park offers breathtaking mountain vistas and a wide range of outdoor activities for families. Take a gondola ride to the top of Sulphur Mountain for panoramic views, and explore the Banff Park Museum to learn about the region's wildlife and history. Lake Louise, with its turquoise waters, is perfect for hiking, canoeing, and picnicking. Families can also enjoy wildlife spotting, go horseback riding, or take a scenic drive along the Icefields Parkway.

Halifax, Nova Scotia:

Halifax, a vibrant coastal city, offers a mix of history, culture, and outdoor adventures. Visit the Maritime Museum of the Atlantic to learn about the city's maritime heritage and the famous Titanic tragedy. Families can enjoy a stroll along the picturesque waterfront boardwalk, where they'll find shops, restaurants, and street performers. The Discovery Centre is a hands-on science museum with interactive exhibits for all ages. A day trip to

Peggy's Cove, with its iconic lighthouse and rugged coastline, is a must for breathtaking scenery.

Ottawa, Ontario:

As Canada's capital, Ottawa is an excellent destination for families interested in history and culture. The Canadian Museum of History provides a fascinating journey through Canada's past, while the Canada Science and Technology Museum offers interactive exhibits on scientific discoveries and innovations. Parliament Hill offers free guided tours and the opportunity to witness the Changing of the Guard ceremony. During winter, families can skate on the Rideau Canal, the world's largest naturally frozen skating rink.

Prince Edward Island:

Known for its red sand beaches, picturesque lighthouses, and Anne of Green Gables, Prince Edward Island is an enchanting destination for families. Explore the Anne of Green Gables Heritage Place, a charming farm that inspired Lucy Maud Montgomery's famous novel. The Green Gables House, a National Historic Site, offers guided tours and activities for children. Families can also enjoy beachcombing, biking along the

Confederation Trail, or experiencing a traditional clam digging adventure.

Canada offers a wealth of family-friendly destinations that combine natural beauty, cultural experiences, and educational opportunities. From the stunning landscapes of Banff National Park to the historic charm of Quebec City and the vibrant cities of Vancouver and Toronto, families are sure to find an abundance of activities and attractions to suit their interests. By exploring these family-friendly destinations, visitors to Canada can create lasting memories while discovering the country's diverse and captivating offerings.

•Activities for Kids

Canada, with its vast landscapes, rich cultural heritage, and diverse wildlife, is a wonderful destination for family travel. From coast to coast, this expansive country offers a plethora of activities that will keep children entertained, engaged, and educated. In this comprehensive Canada travel guide, we will explore a range of fun and educational activities for kids, ensuring that your family's visit to Canada is both enjoyable and memorable.

Explore Natural Wonders:

Canada is renowned for its breathtaking natural wonders, and exploring these sites can be an awe-inspiring experience for children. From the majestic Niagara Falls in Ontario to the stunning Rocky Mountains in Alberta and British Columbia, nature offers endless opportunities for exploration and adventure. Families can engage in activities such as hiking, wildlife spotting, camping, and even taking scenic boat rides to fully appreciate Canada's natural beauty.

Discover National Parks:

Canada is home to numerous national parks that showcase its diverse ecosystems and wildlife. For example, Banff National Park, located in Alberta, offers opportunities for families to spot bears, elk, and mountain goats while surrounded by stunning alpine landscapes. Other notable parks include

Jasper National Park, Pacific Rim National Park, and Gros Morne National Park. These parks often have interactive visitor centers, guided tours, and educational programs designed specifically for children.

Immerse in Indigenous Culture:

Canada has a rich Indigenous heritage, and learning about the traditions and customs of the First Nations can be a captivating experience for kids. Cultural centers, such as the Royal British Columbia Museum in Victoria, British Columbia, and the Canadian Museum of History in Gatineau, Quebec, offer exhibits and interactive displays that educate visitors about Indigenous cultures. Additionally, attending powwows, storytelling sessions, and traditional ceremonies can provide children with a deeper understanding of Canada's Indigenous peoples.

Visit Museums and Science Centers:

Canada boasts numerous museums and science centers that cater to children's curiosity and thirst for knowledge. The Ontario Science Centre in Toronto, for instance, offers hands-on exhibits, interactive workshops, and IMAX films, covering topics ranging from space exploration to human anatomy. Other notable institutions include the Canadian Museum for Human Rights in Winnipeg and the Canadian Museum of Nature in Ottawa, where children can explore exhibits on dinosaurs, wildlife, and the natural world.

Engage in Winter Activities:

Canada's long and snowy winters offer a plethora of exciting activities for kids. Ice skating is a beloved Canadian pastime, and many cities, including Ottawa, Montreal, and Vancouver, have outdoor rinks that are open to the public. Families can also enjoy winter sports such as skiing, snowboarding, and snowshoeing at renowned resorts like Whistler in British Columbia and Mont-Tremblant in Quebec. For a truly unique experience, a visit to the Quebec Winter Carnival in Quebec City provides a chance to embrace the vibrant culture and festivities associated with winter.

Discover Marine Life:

Canada's extensive coastline provides opportunities for children to learn about marine life and ocean conservation. The Vancouver Aquarium in British Columbia is a popular attraction, offering interactive displays and programs where kids can witness marine animals up close. On the East Coast, a visit to the Atlantic Canada region allows families to go whale watching, visit fishing villages, and explore the Bay of Fundy, known for its incredible tides and diverse marine ecosystems.

Participate in Cultural Festivals:
Canada is a multicultural nation that celebrates its diversity through various cultural festivals and events. Attending festivals like the Calgary Stampede in Alberta, the Toronto International Film Festival in Ontario, or the Montreal International Jazz Festival in Quebec can be exciting for children and provide them with an opportunity to experience different cultures, cuisines, and performances.

Explore Historical Sites:
Canada has a rich history, and visiting historical sites can be both educational and entertaining for children. Sites such as the Fortress of Louisbourg in Nova Scotia, the Citadel National Historic Site in Halifax, and the Old Quebec City offer a glimpse into Canada's past through engaging reenactments, guided tours, and interactive exhibits. Children can immerse themselves in the stories of early settlers, explorers, and Indigenous communities that shaped the country.

Canada offers a wide range of activities that cater to children's interests while providing educational and memorable experiences. Whether exploring the country's natural wonders, engaging with Indigenous culture, visiting museums and science centers, participating in winter activities, discovering marine life, celebrating cultural festivals, or exploring historical sites, there is something for every child in this vast and diverse country. By incorporating these activities into your family's travel itinerary, you can create a truly enriching and enjoyable experience for your kids in Canada.

•*Practical Tips for Traveling with Children*

Traveling with children can be an enriching and memorable experience for families. Canada, with its diverse landscapes, vibrant cities, and family-friendly attractions, offers numerous opportunities for an unforgettable vacation.

However, to ensure a smooth and enjoyable trip, it's important to plan ahead and consider the unique needs of traveling with children. In this comprehensive travel guide, we will provide practical tips and advice for families traveling with children in Canada.

Pre-Trip Planning:
Research Destinations: Begin by researching family-friendly destinations in Canada. Consider factors such as proximity to amenities, safety, and the availability of child-friendly activities.
Travel Documents: Ensure that all family members have valid passports, and check if any additional documents or visas are required for entry into Canada.
Travel Insurance: Purchase travel insurance that covers medical emergencies, trip cancellations, and lost luggage. It's important to have peace of mind in case of any unforeseen circumstances.
Health Precautions: Consult your healthcare provider regarding any necessary vaccinations or preventive measures before traveling to Canada.
Choosing Accommodations:
Family-Friendly Hotels: Look for hotels that cater specifically to families, with amenities such as

spacious rooms, play areas, swimming pools, and babysitting services.

Vacation Rentals: Consider renting a family-friendly vacation home or apartment. This option provides more space, a kitchen for preparing meals, and the convenience of a home away from home.

Packing Essentials:

Clothing: Pack appropriate clothing for the weather conditions in Canada. Layers are essential as temperatures can vary significantly across different regions and seasons.

Travel Gear: Bring necessary travel gear such as a stroller, baby carrier, car seat, and a lightweight foldable crib if required. These items can make your journey more comfortable and convenient.

Snacks and Entertainment: Pack a variety of healthy snacks, drinks, and entertainment options for your children to keep them engaged during long journeys or wait times.

Safety Considerations:

Child Identification: Ensure that each child has some form of identification, such as an ID card or wristband with contact information.

Car Safety: If you plan to rent a car, make sure you have appropriate car seats for your children's age and size. Familiarize yourself with the local traffic rules and regulations.

Water Safety: Canada is known for its beautiful lakes and rivers. Ensure your children are supervised at all times near water bodies, and consider using life jackets for added safety.

Transportation Tips:

Public Transportation: Familiarize yourself with the public transportation options available in your destination. Many cities in Canada have well-developed public transit systems that are stroller-friendly.

Road Trips: If you plan to embark on a road trip, plan frequent breaks to allow children to stretch their legs and explore. Bring along games, books, and other forms of entertainment to keep them engaged during the journey.

Family-Friendly Activities:

National Parks: Canada is renowned for its breathtaking national parks. Research child-friendly hikes, nature trails, and educational programs that will captivate your children's curiosity and provide them with an opportunity to learn about Canada's natural wonders.

Museums and Science Centers: Many cities in Canada offer museums and science centers with interactive exhibits designed to engage children of all ages. Research these attractions in advance and check for any special events or exhibitions.

Wildlife Encounters: Canada is home to diverse wildlife. Consider visiting wildlife reserves, aquariums, or zoos where your children can observe and learn about native animals while respecting their natural habitats.

Food and Dining:

Child-Friendly Restaurants: Look for restaurants that offer children's menus or have a reputation for being family-friendly. These establishments often provide high chairs, booster seats, and activities to keep children entertained.

Dietary Considerations: If your child has any specific dietary restrictions or allergies, communicate this to the staff at restaurants or accommodations in advance. Ensure you have necessary snacks or food alternatives readily available.

Weather Preparedness:

Extreme Temperatures: Canada experiences varying weather conditions, from cold winters to hot summers. Pack appropriate clothing and gear, such as hats, sunscreen, mittens, and jackets, to ensure your children are comfortable in different climates.

Rainy Days: Be prepared for rainy weather by carrying waterproof jackets, umbrellas, and indoor activity options to keep children entertained during inclement weather.

Cultural Sensitivity:

Teach Cultural Etiquette: Educate your children about Canadian customs and cultural norms, such as being polite, respecting personal space, and observing local traditions.

Indigenous Culture: Canada has a rich Indigenous heritage. Research and visit cultural centers or events where your children can learn about and appreciate Indigenous traditions, art, and history.

Traveling with children in Canada can be a truly rewarding experience. By following these practical tips and planning ahead, you can ensure a safe, enjoyable, and memorable journey for the entire family. Remember to remain flexible, prioritize your children's needs, and create lasting memories as you explore the wonders of Canada together.

Chapter Ten

Conclusion

•*Summary*

This is a guidebook that invites travelers to delve into the wonders of this vast and diverse country. By combining practical information, local insights, and inspiring recommendations, it aims to help visitors create memorable experiences and forge lasting connections with the people, landscapes, and cultures of Canada. Whether you are a first-time traveler or a seasoned adventurer, this guidebook is an essential tool for unlocking the secrets and treasures of this captivating destination. Get ready

• *Final Thoughts*

Canada, the land of vast landscapes, diverse cultures, and breathtaking beauty, has always been a coveted destination for travelers around the world. From the snow-capped peaks of the Rocky Mountains to the vibrant multicultural cities like Toronto and Vancouver, Canada offers an array of experiences that leave a lasting impression on anyone fortunate enough to visit. As I reflect upon my own journey to this magnificent country, I am overwhelmed with a sense of wonder and gratitude. In this final reflection, I will delve into the enchanting aspects of traveling to Canada, recounting the highlights and sharing my personal insights from the experience.

Natural Splendors:
Canada's natural wonders are nothing short of awe-inspiring. The country boasts a diverse range of landscapes, from the majestic Canadian Rockies to the pristine lakes and dense forests of Algonquin Provincial Park. Witnessing the vastness of the Niagara Falls or taking a boat tour through the fjords of British Columbia leaves an indelible mark on one's soul. The opportunity to explore the expansive wilderness, breathe in the crisp mountain air, and encounter wildlife in their natural habitats is an experience that cannot be replicated. Canada's commitment to environmental preservation is

evident in its numerous national parks, providing visitors with an unspoiled oasis of tranquility.

Cultural Tapestry:

One of the most striking aspects of traveling to Canada is the celebration of cultural diversity. From the French-speaking province of Quebec to the vibrant Asian communities in Vancouver, Canada is a melting pot of cultures, traditions, and languages. Embracing multiculturalism, Canadians are known for their warmth and acceptance, creating an inclusive society that makes visitors feel welcome. Experiencing the culinary delights of different cultures, attending festivals showcasing indigenous art and music, and immersing oneself in the rich heritage of various communities offers a profound insight into the fabric of Canadian society.

Urban Marvels:

Beyond its natural splendors, Canada's cities captivate with their modern infrastructure, artistic expressions, and vibrant energy. Toronto, the country's largest city, exudes a cosmopolitan atmosphere with its towering skyscrapers, eclectic neighborhoods, and world-class dining. Vancouver, nestled between the Pacific Ocean and the mountains, showcases a perfect blend of urban life and natural beauty. Exploring the cobblestone streets of Old Quebec City takes you back in time, while the multicultural neighborhoods of Montreal offer a fusion of old-world charm and contemporary vibrancy. Each city has its unique character, inviting visitors to immerse themselves in the local culture and embrace the fast-paced urban lifestyle.

Adventure and Recreation:
Canada is a playground for adventure enthusiasts. Whether it's skiing in Whistler, hiking in Banff National Park, or kayaking along the coast of Nova Scotia, the country offers endless opportunities for outdoor activities. The Great Trail, spanning over 24,000 kilometers, provides hikers, bikers, and nature lovers with an unparalleled experience, traversing diverse landscapes from coast to coast. In the winter months, Canada transforms into a winter wonderland, where one can indulge in activities like ice skating on frozen lakes, dog sledding, and even catching a glimpse of the mesmerizing Northern Lights. The sense of freedom and connection with nature that accompanies these adventures is truly invigorating.

Reflections and Personal Growth:

Traveling to Canada has not only provided me with unforgettable memories but has also enriched my personal growth. It has taught me the value of embracing diversity, fostering an appreciation for different cultures and perspectives. Engaging in conversations with locals, learning about their customs and traditions, and immersing myself in unfamiliar surroundings has broadened my horizons and cultivated a sense of empathy. The sheer beauty of Canada's landscapes has reminded me of the importance of environmental conservation, prompting me to make more sustainable choices in my own life. Moreover, navigating through unfamiliar territories and experiencing new challenges has instilled in me a sense of resilience and adaptability.

In conclusion, embarking on a journey to Canada is an experience that transcends mere tourism. It is an immersive adventure that awakens the senses, rejuvenates the spirit, and fosters personal growth. The natural wonders, cultural tapestry, vibrant cities, and boundless opportunities for adventure come together to create an extraordinary destination. Canada's commitment to inclusivity, environmental preservation, and quality of life sets it apart as a place that not only provides unforgettable experiences but also leaves a lasting impact on those fortunate enough to explore its vast landscapes. As I reflect upon my own journey, I am filled with gratitude for the memories and lessons that Canada has bestowed upon me. I encourage all wanderers and seekers of the extraordinary to embark on their own journey to Canada and discover the wonders that await them.

Printed in Great Britain
by Amazon

36938981R00185